YOUR

NEW

BUSINESS:

A Personal

Plan for

Success

by Charles L. Martin, Ph.D.

THE
CRISP
SMALL BUSINESS &
ENTREPRENEURSHIP
SERIES

CREDITS

Editor: Beverly Manber

Layout/Design: University Graphics

Cover Design: Kathleen Gadway

Library of Congress 92-054374
ISBN-1-56052-170-8

INTRODUCTION TO THE SERIES

This series of books is intended to inform and assist those of you who are in the beginning stages of starting a new small business venture or who are considering such an undertaking.

It is because you are confident of your abilities that you are taking this step. These books will provide additional information and support along the way.

Not every new business will succeed. The more information you have about budgeting, cash flow management, accounts receivables, marketing and employee management, the better prepared you will be for the inevitable pitfalls.

A unique feature of the *Crisp Small Business & Entrepreneurship Series* is the personal involvement exercises, which give you many opportunities to immediately apply the concepts presented to your own business.

In each book in the series, these exercises take the form of "Your Turn", a checklist to confirm your understanding of the concept just presented and "Ask Yourself...", a series of chapter-ending questions, designed to evaluate your overall understanding or commitment.

In addition, numerous case studies are included, and each book is cross-referenced to others in the series and to other publications.

BOOKS IN THE SERIES

► **Operating a Really Small Business**
Betty M. Bivins

► **Budgeting: A Primer for Entrepreneurs**
Terry Dickey

► **Getting a Business Loan: Your Step-By-Step Guide**
Orlando J. Antonini

► **Nobody Gets Rich Working for Somebody Else:
An Entrepreneur's Guide**
Roger Fritz

► **Marketing Strategies for Small Business**
Richard F. Gerson, Ph.D.

► **Financial Basics for Small Business Success**
James O. Gill

► **Extending Credit and Collecting Cash:
A Small Business Guide**
Lynn Harrison

► **Avoiding Mistakes in Your New Business**
David Karlson, Ph.D.

► **Buying Your First Franchise:
The Least You Need to Know**
Rebecca Luhn, Ph.D.

► **Buying a Business: Tips for the First-Time Buyer**
Ronald J. McGregor

► **Your New Business: A Personal Plan for Success**
Charles L. Martin, Ph.D.

► **Managing the Family Business:
A Guide for Success**
Marshall W. Northington, Ph.D.

TABLE OF CONTENTS

CONTENTS (continued)

CONTENTS

CONTENTS (continued)

CHAPTER ONE

THE ENTREPRENEURIAL SPIRIT

DO YOU HAVE THE SPIRIT?

"It is easy to find fault with a new idea.
It is easier to say it can't be done, than to try.
Thus, it is through the fear of failure,
That some men create their own Hell."

— E. Jacob Taylor

Part of the American dream many of us share is to someday own our own business. As opportunities abound for owning and operating small businesses, for most of us the dream is within reach. About 675,000 businesses are started each year. Most of them are small businesses, founded by people who are probably not unlike you. There are currently more than 17 million small, nonfarm businesses in the U.S. By the year 2000, that number is expected to grow to 25 million. That will be 25 million small businesses that began with an entrepreneur's dream and desire to succeed.

Here are a few more statistics about small business and entrepreneurship in the U.S. that suggest *small* business is not so small after all:

► 87 percent of all businesses employ less than 20 employees.

► More than 27 percent of all workers work in businesses that employ less than 20 employees, and 56 percent of the labor force work in businesses employing fewer than 100 employees.

► The size of the *average* business is decreasing: the number of businesses is growing faster than the Gross National Product.

► Entrepreneurs are innovative: patents issued to individuals are on the rise—jumping 37 percent between 1986 and 1990.

► Small businesses access world markets: 60 percent of firms who successfully export abroad are small businesses employing fewer than 100 workers.

► About 70 percent of the small businesses started this year are predicted to fail within five years.

► Despite the failures, in the 1990s, the number of small businesses is expected to grow by more than 40 percent.

► In the late 1970s, about 1,000 college students were enrolled in entrepreneurship courses. Today, several hundred colleges and universities offer entrepreneurship courses for thousands of students. One innovative course at the University of Michigan requires students to find their own seed money and to start a serious business during the semester. Some schools, such as Wichita State University, have programs in which students can major in entrepreneurship.

To a budding entrepreneur, small business offers the opportunity for a personally satisfying and rewarding endeavor—a chance to *battle the world*, to build something from scratch, to control one's destiny, to be independent and work autonomously, to satisfy a genuine need in the community, to grow as an individual, and to have no one else limit the business' horizons.

UNDERSTANDING THE RISKS

The glamorous and exciting lure of starting a small business blinds many people to the stark realities of entrepreneurship. The risks and disadvantages should not be quietly dismissed or discounted—they are very real. For example, between 55,000 and 65,000 small businesses fail each year. Many of these failing businesses take with them the life savings—and often the self-esteem—of their founders. If past trends continue, about 70 percent of all small businesses started this year will fail before beginning their sixth year of operation. Of the 30 percent that survive, many will be less financially rewarding than originally envisioned.

Beyond the financial risk of insolvency, numerous personal drawbacks face those who start their own small business. Successful small business owners, for example, rarely enjoy the luxury of a standard eight-hour/five-day week. In fact, a recent study conducted by the National Association for the Self-Employed found that the typical small business owner works an average of 52.5 hours per week. This compares to only 43.5 hours for the work force as a whole. As an owner of a small retail clothing store explained, "Owning your own business means working Saturdays forever." Moreover, when a new business is in its infancy, 80-hour work weeks are not uncommon.

The responsibility of running the business lies ultimately with the proprietor—a role that can be quite stressful and lonely. Often the most difficult decisions and the most unpleasant tasks cannot be delegated. And, unlike working for larger corporations, there may be no supervisors or mentors from whom to seek help.

The time-consuming and stressful nature of owning a business frequently affects proprietors' families as well. Small business owners are likely to have less stable marriages than the rest of the public. Family members may be expected to work in the business, sometimes involuntarily; business disputes may lead to family disputes; family vacations and other plans may be postponed or altered when business plans take precedence. Planning the family budget may be a stressful process, given the uncertain income generated by the business and the anxiety that results from never knowing how much money to take out of the business for personal use, and how much to reinvest in the business.

Many small business owners find they are less independent than they initially believed. In many respects, customers, suppliers and government agencies become the proprietor's new *bosses*. These constituencies may be equally demanding, if not more, than previous employers.

Finally, some owners grow to hate their businesses and/or their partners. They may feel trapped—unable to sell the business or dissolve the partnership as quickly as they would like.

Starting a business is not something to be undertaken casually or lightly. Clearly there are opportunities for successful small business ventures, but anyone considering going into business for him or herself is well-advised to carefully weigh the pros and cons. In other words, look before you leap.

SUCCESS FACTORS: BEATING THE ODDS

Hopefully, you are not too discouraged after reading the last few paragraphs. It is useful to understand the potential downside of venturing into your own business. Being sensitive to the negatives can help you prepare to beat the odds and can enhance the likelihood of your profitable business venture. Preparation begins when you examine the factors associated with successful business start-ups. Success factors include several elements discussed below: the personal characteristics and prior experiences of successful entrepreneurs, a winning idea, a plan and sufficient funds.

Personal Characteristics

Although most leaders and educators in entrepreneurship believe that the principles of entrepreneurship can be learned, research suggests that some personal traits of entrepreneurs seem to develop over a long period of time; these business people almost seem to be born with entrepreneurial tendencies. Not surprisingly, for example, one study found that entrepreneurs tend to be extremely optimistic. They believe their businesses will prosper over time and do not fear failure. If they are forced to close their businesses, rather than believing they failed, they see themselves as only temporarily detoured on their way to eventual success in another venture. Most successful entrepreneurs have histories of not quitting—they have often *failed* several times before they establish their winning businesses.

Similarly, entrepreneurs seem to have a high tolerance for risk and uncertainty. Such tolerance helps them to confront problems and opportunities, and to act without unnecessary hesitation. They do not dwell upon the possibility of making a bad decision, though they are not immune to mistakes and their consequences. Many seem to thrive upon risk and uncertainty, and often prefer to move ahead with a project, rather than to wait for additional information that might reduce the risk.

Entrepreneurs tend to have a high need for power and/or achievement. They like to be in control of their personal destinies and that of their businesses. They get tremendous satisfaction from building their new businesses from scratch, from seeing their new products or services introduced in the marketplace, and from seeing the impact of their other business decisions.

Given the long hours and hard work required to build a new business, entrepreneurs tend to be in good health. They are not afraid to work long hours—often taking pride in their willingness and ability to work. And, because they have to work with so many constituencies such as employees, customers and suppliers, they tend to have above average interpersonal communications skills; they tend to get along fairly well with other people.

Entrepreneurial traits have negative implications in some instances. For example, many entrepreneurs have such a strong need to stay in control and to be involved with every decision that they find it difficult to delegate responsibility to employees. An entrepreneur's failure to delegate prevents employees from reaching their maximum potential. This ultimately inhibits the business' ability to grow. Conversely, an entrepreneur with a strong need for achievement may push the business to grow too fast—creating unnecessary risks, for example, misreading the marketplace, expecting too much of employees, or draining assets needed to finance the rapid growth.

Prior Experience

Prior experience in an industry or type of business is generally a plus, although it may not be mandatory. Entrepreneur Ray Kroc, credited with parlaying McDonald's into a worldwide hamburger empire, gained experience in the fast food industry by selling milk shake machines to dining establishments. Dave Thomas, Wendy's founder, gained valuable experience by working first for Kentucky Fried Chicken.

It is common for an individual to learn about an industry or type of business by working first for someone else and then starting his or her own operation. Sometimes the former employer becomes a partner in the new venture; at other times s/he becomes a competitor. In either case, the experience is beneficial if, for no other reason, the entrepreneur learns from the mistakes of the former employer. In most instances, prior experience helps the prospective entrepreneur learn the *ins and outs* and idiosyncrasies of the industry—e.g., what are the normal operating procedures, who are the most reliable suppliers, what is a *fair* price for raw materials and supplies, what customers like and do not like, and so on. This does not mean that the new business necessarily has to emulate existing businesses, but knowledge obtained through prior experience in the industry helps the entrepreneur know how to best deviate from established norms.

Winning Idea

A couple of years ago, a frustrated owner of a small, struggling clothing store in northern Texas asked me how he could compete with the larger department stores in his community. The larger stores were undercutting his prices and outselling him. His low volume prevented him from commanding deep discounts from his suppliers, so he could not compete on the basis of price. Unfortunately, he did not feel he could compete on the basis of customer service either, since he believed most consumers would not pay for improved service. He did not see a way he could successfully compete against his larger competitors.

As he explained his dilemma, it became clear that he had not thought out his business concept carefully before opening his store. Apparently, he believed that because the demand for clothing was already well established, his store would automatically reap a fair share of the community's clothing business. He failed to realize that winning business ideas contain some competitive edge or differential advantage. A successful business has to be superior to the competition in at least one way, if not in several ways.

Offering a unique product or service that competitors do not offer is one way to create a competitive edge. Lower prices, higher quality, more variety, a more convenient location, a wider range of services, a more knowledgeable and courteous staff, stronger guarantees and more liberal return policies are among the many other options. It is important to note that the distinction between a business and its competitors creates a competitive edge only when the difference is noted and valued by potential customers. There is no such thing as a better mousetrap if consumers are unaware of its existence or if they are satisfied with the mousetraps they have been purchasing for years.

A Plan

Successful businesses do not just happen. They become successful because someone had a vision for the business, which they translated into a workable plan. Every successful business venture must have a plan—a blueprint, of sorts, to safely guide the business toward its objectives. Planning helps identify the issues that must be addressed to establish and operate the business. A well-written plan also serves as a useful communication tool that clearly conveys the entrepreneur's vision to interested stakeholders—prospective partners, employees, suppliers and investors. In short, as the saying goes, "if you fail to plan, plan to fail." We will discuss the planning process in detail in later chapters.

Sufficient Funds

Successful businesses must have sufficient funds, not only to open the doors, but to keep them open for several months as the business is nurtured through its infancy. As the business grows, an ever-increasing amount of capital may be tied-up in raw materials, inventory, supplies and accounts receivables. Juggling the timing of receipts and expenditures, and maintaining access to additional funds as the business grows, are critical to the success of any business.

Recognizing the Pitfalls

Another closely related way to beat the odds is to understand some of the major pitfalls that often lead to business failures. Recognizing these potential problems will help you avoid them. Here are some common pitfalls and specific actions that can be taken to side-step them.[1] We will continue to examine these issues throughout the book.

Pitfalls

► Lack of experience
► Lack of money/capital

---

[1] Sources: *The Pitfalls in Managing a Small Business,* W.H. Kuehn, New York: Dun and Bradstreet, 1973 and "Classic Causes of Entrepreneurial Failure," Roger H. Ford, *Business Perspectives,* Spring 1989, pp. 22-23.

- ► Wrong location
- ► Inventory mismanagement
- ► Too much capital going into fixed assets
- ► Poor credit granting practices
- ► Taking too much personal income
- ► Failing to plan
- ► Having the wrong attitude
- ► Choosing the wrong partners
- ► Not knowing yourself
- ► Having unrealistic expectations

To address these pitfalls

- ► Recognize limitations
- ► Plan properly
- ► Keep records
- ► Watch the balance sheet—not just the profits
- ► Investigate
- ► Cooperate with suppliers and banks
- ► Learn
- ► Utilize professional assistance
- ► Watch your health

DO YOU HAVE WHAT IT TAKES?

> "Real opportunities lie within a person, not outside.
> What lies behind you and what lies before you are
> tiny matters compared to what lies within you."
>
> — *Ralph Waldo Emerson*

As shown below, entrepreneurs have backgrounds that are as
varied as their ventures. Many start their businesses in their
twenties, while others wait a few years. Formal education seems
to be a *plus*, but not absolutely essential.

- Twenty-five percent started their businesses before age 30. Eleven percent were over age 50 when they started theirs.

- Thirty-two percent graduated from high school, but never attended college. Twenty-seven percent earned a Bachelor's degree and/or an advanced college degree.

- Forty-five percent have parents who owned an independent business.

- Forty-six percent had been previously employed in a small business.

- The percentage of minorities in the U.S. who own their own businesses is increasing. These groups lead the way: Korean (10.2%), Asian Indian (7.6%), Japanese (6.6%), Chinese (6.3%), Cuban (6.3%) and Vietnamese (4.9%). Women are also making great strides in entrepreneurship, as shown in the next section.

Female Entrepreneurs

In the late 1960's, Lynn Wilson failed to land a job in a commercial design firm. The executive who denied Wilson's application told her that, if she was hired, Wilson would probably leave in a short time to launch her own business. Before the interview, Lynn Wilson had never considered being an entrepreneur; after the rejection, she decided to give it a try. She began an interior design company from her home, with a $200 investment. By 1990, her Florida company, Lynn Wilson Associates, was tallying annual revenues of more than $250 million.

Most entrepreneurs in the past have been male, but females are making substantial inroads in small business ownership. Lynn Wilson's success story is one of many. Consider these eye-opening statistics:

- About 30 percent of the nation's businesses are women-owned, accounting for almost $280 billion in revenues.

- Most firms owned by women are less than five years old and have four or fewer employees.

► The number of women who own small businesses in the U.S. has increased several times faster than that of men. For example, a 1990 count of 1.3 million sole proprietorships formed since 1987 identified 1.2 million of the businesses owned by women.

► Female entrepreneurs tend to start their businesses about a decade later than male entrepreneurs—usually between the ages of 35 and 45.

► Businesses in retailing, insurance and real estate are popular ventures, started by a high proportion of female entrepreneurs.

Surveys of female entrepreneurs indicate that women go into business for many of the same reasons men do—in search of challenge, flexibility, autonomy in decision-making, and so on. Women are also prompted in instances where the difficulty of shattering the "glass ceiling" barrier in the corporate world is perceived as high.

Research also reveals a few differences between male and female entrepreneurs, once they are in business, although there are far more similarities. For example, one study found that female entrepreneurs were more likely to prefer owning small and stable businesses than were males, implying that women may not be as interested in expanding their businesses. Another study found that female entrepreneurs tend to score lower on factors such as energy level and risk tolerance than do males. This may explain females' satisfaction with operating smaller businesses.

The Moment of Truth

More reliable predictors of successful entrepreneurs involve the assessment of each individual's aptitude and level of motivation. Many educational institutions and some government agencies provide testing services to help prospective entrepreneurs diagnose their strengths and weaknesses. One such program is called GATB—General Aptitude Tests Battery.

A viable alternative to the GATB and similar tests may be to execute an objective self-assessment of your entrepreneurial potential. Robert Schaefer recommends that a self-assessment should begin with your honest answer to the following question:

Knowing what I do about myself, would I hire someone like me to run a business that I have invested my life savings in?[2]

Next, list your work experience, skills and education. This is similar to what you might be asked to do by an employment agency. The list will help you identify weaknesses that you might strengthen with additional preparation.

The Small Business Administration provides a structured self-assessment questionnaire, reproduced below, that will also help you to learn whether you have what it takes to be an entrepreneur. Under each question, check the answer that best reflects the way you feel.

Self-Assessment Questionnaire[3]

Are you a self-starter?

___ I do things on my own. Nobody has to tell me to get going.

___ If someone gets me started, I keep going all right.

___ Easy does it. I don't put myself out until I have to.

Can you lead others?

___ I can get most people to go along when I start doing something.

___ I can give orders if someone tells me what we should do.

___ I let someone else get things moving. Then, I go along if I feel like it.

---

[2] Source: *Starting and Managing a Small Service Business,* Robert A. Schaefer, Washington D.C.: U.S. Small Business Administration, 1986, p. 8.

[3] Source: *Checklist for Going Into Business,* Management Aid #2.016, U.S. Small Business Administration, 1985.

Can you take responsibility?

___ I like to take charge of things and see them through.

___ I'll take over if I have to, but I'd rather let someone else be responsible.

___ There is always some eager beaver around wanting to show how smart he is. I say let him.

How good an organizer are you?

___ I like to have a plan before I start. I'm usually the one to get things lined up when the group wants to do something.

___ I do all right unless things get too confused. Then I quit.

___ You get all set and then something comes along and presents too many problems. So I just take things as they come.

How good a worker are you?

___ I can keep going as long as I need to. I don't mind working hard for something I want.

___ I'll work hard for a while, but when I've had enough. that's it.

___ I can't see that hard work gets you anywhere.

Can you make decisions?

___ I can make up my mind in a hurry if I have to. It usually turns out OK, too.

___ I can if I have plenty of time. If I have to make up my mind fast, later I think I should have decided the other way.

___ I don't like to be the one who has to decide things.

Can people trust what you say?

___ You bet they can. I don't say things I don't mean.

___ I try to be on the level most of the time, but sometimes I just say what's easiest.

___ Why bother if the other fellow doesn't know the difference?

Can you stick with it?

___ If I make up my mind to do something, I don't let anything stop me.

___ I usually finish what I start—if it goes well.

___ If it doesn't go right away, I quit. Why beat your brains out?

How good is your health?

___ I never run down!

___ I have enough energy for most things I want to do.

___ I seem to run out of energy sooner than most of my friends seem to.

To interpret the results of the self-assessment exercise, note whether most of your checks are beside the first choices. If so, congratulations! You probably have what it takes to own and operate a business. If many of your checks are beside the second choices, consider teaming-up with a partner who can offset your weaker areas. Research suggests that teaming-up with a competent partner will usually increase your chances of business success. If you have checked many of the third responses, you might pat yourself on the back for being honest, and seriously consider working for someone else.

Before moving to the next chapter, here is a quick checklist of ten ingredients for entrepreneurial success, offered by James R. Paul, CEO for Coastal Corporation.[4] Do you identify with these characteristics? Do you have what it takes? Do you have the entrepreneurial spirit?

► Hard work: consistently practice plain, old-fashioned hard work.

► Focus: you must be able to concentrate on what you do best.

► Good ideas: look for good ideas like a dog looks for a fire plug. Every day, look for new ideas, new methods, new ways to improve, to grow—new ways to raise productivity, to find new customers, to control costs and to eliminate bureaucracy.

► Flexibility: flexibility succeeds.

► Adaptability to change: adapt to change, and learn to anticipate it.

► Sales: you must be able to get others to buy into your ideas.

► Confidence: successful people ooze confidence from every pore.

► Balance: maintain a balance between detail and general thinking; a sense of perspective is important.

► Assertiveness: successful people use it to their advantage.

► Improvement: constantly improve yourself and your company.

---

[4] Source: Speech by James R. Paul, March 27, 1991, Wichita, Kansas: Wichita State University, Center for Entrepreneurship

ASK YOURSELF

► Do you want to own your own business? If so, why?

► How do successful entrepreneurs differ from other people?

► In what ways are you entrepreneurial and in what ways are you *not* entrepreneurial? Do you believe you would be successful as an entrepreneur?

► Why do many small businesses fail? If you start your own business, how will you increase your business' likelihood of success?

► Knowing what you do about yourself, would you hire someone like you to run a business for you? Why or why not?

CHAPTER TWO

SIZING UP
THE OPTIONS

WHAT ARE YOUR OPTIONS?

Once you have made a personal commitment to own your own business, examine the numerous options available to make it happen. You might start from scratch and create a new business. Possibilities include businesses that may be run from your home, such as the interior design business that Lynn Wilson started. Another obvious option would be to create a small business, such as a retail store, that would require a separate location away from your home. Visit almost any mall and you will find businesses whose owners began their businesses this way. Still another possibility is to buy an existing business from the current owner(s). And, many of today's entrepreneurs are buying local franchises from nationally known companies such as Hardee's (fast food), Western Sizzlin' (restaurants), Jazzercise (fitness centers), Fantastic Sams (hair care centers) and Maaco (auto painting).

Which of these options is best for you? That depends. We will now examine each alternative in greater depth.

FRANCHISING

Purchasing a franchise from an established, reputable company can be an attractive alternative for budding entrepreneurs who have never before owned a business. More than 550,000 franchise outlets in the U.S. today attest to the popularity of this business option. Typically, franchisors have fine-tuned the business operation before attempting to sell franchise units; it is in their best interest to provide helpful assistance to franchisees, which minimizes mistakes and mishaps. Another advantage is the instant name recognition and reputation a franchise inherits from the parent company. If you enter the highly competitive fast food industry, for example, it may take years to establish an independent operation named McFred's or McBob's, but you will probably have customers streaming through your door from day one if you purchase a McDonald's franchise.

Despite the advantages of franchise ownership, consider these potential disadvantages. If you are very independent or very creative, you may not be happy as a franchisee. That is, following the franchisor's detailed policies and procedures may resemble a job where you work for someone else—a situation you may be trying to avoid. And, like any new business venture, franchise opportunities should be evaluated carefully. Some are far better opportunities for the franchisor than for the franchisee.

One useful source of information to begin researching franchise opportunities is *Entrepreneur* magazine. One recent issue, for example, listed and ranked 1,035 franchises. It provided start-up costs, franchise fees, royalties, availability of financing, number of franchise units, required experience and each franchisor's address. The International Franchise Association, located at 1350 New York Avenue, NW, Suite 900, Washington, D.C. 20005, is another source, as is the Small Business Administration (SBA). The SBA's recommendations for evaluating franchise opportunities are listed below.

Evaluating Franchise Opportunities[5]

Who is the franchisor?

► How long has the franchisor been in the industry?

How long has the firm granted franchises?

► How many franchises are there? How many are in your area?

► What is the franchisor's attitude toward you? Is the firm concerned about your qualifications? Has the franchisor tried to rush you to sign the agreement?

► Are franchisees required to purchase supplies from the franchisor? If so, are prices competitive with other suppliers?

► What, if any, restrictions apply to competition with other franchisees?

► What are the terms covering renewal rights and reselling the franchise?

► What is the reputation and image of the franchisor and his products?

---

[5]Source: *Evaluating Franchise Opportunities*, U.S. Small Business Administration, Management Aid #7.007, 1985

Investigate the above questions by:

- ► Visiting the franchisor's headquarters.
- ► Asking the franchisor for a copy of the F.T.C.-required disclosure document.
- ► Talking to . . .
  - — Current franchisees
  - — Small Business Administration
  - — Federal Trade Commission
  - — Better Business Bureau
  - — Chamber of Commerce
  - — International Franchise Association
  - — Your lawyer
  - — Your accountant

BUYING AN EXISTING BUSINESS

On balance, buying an existing business is probably less risky than starting a similar sized business on your own, but may be more risky than purchasing a franchise. *Before* you make a commitment to purchase an existing business, you have the opportunity to observe its operations, talk to its customers and suppliers, scrutinize the business' records, and learn from current owners and managers. If you do not like what you discover about the business, you can examine others until you find one that represents an attractive opportunity, at a reasonable price.

Still, when considering the purchase of an existing business, there are plenty of pitfalls and obstacles to avoid. If your investigation of the business "opportunity" is incomplete, or if it yields inaccurate or misleading information, you may find yourself buying someone else's headaches. The time you invest studying any business carefully before purchasing it is time well spent. During your inquiry, seek answers to key questions from multiple sources such as employees, suppliers, customers, experts in the industry, trade associations and even competitors. In other words, do not rely solely on the information the current owner provides. And, before proceeding very far in the investigation process, it is a good idea to team up with an attorney and an accountant. They will help you interpret the information you collect, favorably structure the sale, and eventually pinpoint a number of detailed issues for you to consider.

During the early stages of the business investigation process, focus on the fundamental issues. There are a myriad of details to address before you finalize the sale. Do not let these secondary concerns distract your attention from the *big picture*. The fundamental questions you should ask yourself are: 1) Why am I interested in buying this business? 2) Why is the existing owner(s) interested in selling? 3) Precisely what is for sale? and 4) What is the value of the business?

Assessing Your Interest

What is it about the business that aroused your interest in buying it? Perhaps you responded to an intriguing classified advertisement announcing the sale, or to the owner's persuasive personal presentation. Maybe you have always wanted to operate this type of business. Possibly you have been impressed with the business as one of its customers or suppliers.

Whatever the reason for your interest, assess whether the interest is genuine. Your personal commitment will usually have to be much greater than that required to work for someone else. That is, how enthusiastic are you about owning the business? Are you likely to be equally enthusiastic a year from now? Five years? Ten years?

For some entrepreneurs, the lure of profits may be sufficiently motivating. Others may need an additional fascination with the business. For example, will you enjoy working in the business? Is there too much—or not enough—desk work or unpredictability that you might find stressful or boring? Will you find it satisfying to interact with the business' customers, employees and suppliers? Are you *turned on* by the business' products and services? In short, do not let anyone else talk you into buying a business that is not right for you. The financial, time and psychological costs of buying a business are too high to let others set your personal criteria for buying a business. It is ultimately *your* decision.

The Seller's Motivations

If a business opportunity sounds too good to be true, it may *not* be true. Before buying a business, try to learn why the owner wants to sell. Is he or she approaching retirement, having health problems, bored with the business, in need of cash for other ventures or for personal reasons? Or, is the owner simply *trying to escape a failing business,* jumping ship before it sinks, so to speak? There are many legitimate reasons for selling a business that should sound no alarm, but if the business is failing, find out why. Can you attribute the failure to the existing management's lack of managerial skills? Has the owner neglected the business, refusing to invest the time and capital to keep it profitable? Or has the competition gained an advantage in the marketplace with a superior location, improved technology or lower prices? Has customer demand fallen because of shoddy merchandise or poor service? Even if the business appears to be profitable today, will impending events, such as a copyright or lease expiration, have a drastic effect on tomorrow's profits?

It is often difficult to identify precise reasons why the business is suffering, but the is ue can not be ignored. Nor should a failing business be avoided automatically. Sinking businesses can often be purchased for very little money and may have high profit potentials. For example, I know of an individual who inherited a mausoleum from a relative. The benefactor knew virtually nothing about the business or the industry. Understandably, he struggled to keep the business afloat, and eventually sold it to individuals who were more knowledgeable and able to revitalize profitability.

Again, if the prospective business is currently unprofitable, assess why it is not making money. Then you will be able to better estimate the likelihood of turning the business around. With some businesses, paying more attention to the day-to-day details of the operation will help affect the turnaround. In other situations, stepping-up the marketing effort may be called for. Renovating the facility, remodeling, redecorating or thoroughly cleaning the premises may have a tremendous effect in some businesses. These types of changes are very realistic and very doable (i.e., they are controllable).

Other problems plaguing profitability may be much less controllable, at least in the short-term. As alluded to earlier, competitors may have gained some strategic advantage that you may be unable to overcome. Demand for the firm's products may have evaporated because the products are completely obsolete—today there are considerably fewer manufacturers of slide rules than twenty years ago. Or perhaps the business' reputation in the community or industry is so poor that almost no level of marketing efforts will coax previously alienated customers to return. With some exceptions, these insurmountable problems represent bona fide reasons not to buy the business, although there may be some exceptions. For example, it may be feasible to purchase part of the business' assets—such as manufacturing or office equipment—when establishing another business in a different location.

What Is For Sale?

What sounds initially like a bright business opportunity may lose its luster after you learn what the sale does and does not entail. Many businesses, for example, do not own the building or real estate where they are located, which affects the value of the business. In fact, it is not uncommon for a business to lease much of its equipment and own very few assets. Even if very few assets are leased, it may not be obvious if some items are to be part of the transaction. Clearly determine whether or not inventories, supplies, furniture and fixtures, trucks, etc., are included in the sale.

Many aspects of the business will be less tangible than physical assets, but no less important to clarify. Accounts receivables, accounts payable and other liabilities, unfilled customer orders, agreements with employees, patents, copyrights and customer lists are some of the intangibles that may significantly impact the business' current value and future profitability.

Another intangible factor that may not be part of the business, per se, but may be a vital component of the transaction, is an agreement not to compete. In other words, is the current owner willing to agree not to open a similar, competing business within a specified number of miles, or within a specified time period, or both? Such an agreement can be extremely critical to service businesses such as bookkeeping services, hair care centers, lawn care businesses, travel agencies, dental practices and auto repair garages. These businesses rely heavily on the expertise and skills of the individual providing the service. Knowing this, satisfied customers are likely to view the service provider and the business as one and the same. If they learn that the former owner opened a new competing business across the street, they may be reluctant to shift their allegiance to the new proprietor.

Valuing the Business

> "What's the business worth?...There're hundreds of answers, and no answers."
>
> — *Robert F. Klueger*

One important question I am frequently asked is, "How much is the business worth?" It is a fair question to ask before deciding how much to offer the business' present owner. And, as Robert F. Klueger suggests, it is not easily answered. Even the IRS has not developed an ironclad formula for determining a business' worth. There is really only one formula that is defensible: *the value of a business is the amount an informed buyer will pay to an informed and willing seller.* Unfortunately, this rule-of-thumb does not provide much guidance, except to imply that the purchase price of a business is always negotiable.

Several methods and tools have been developed to estimate the worth of a business; but these should only be used as starting points, to be adjusted up or down depending upon subjective factors such as: the long term profit potential or risk the business faces; how the sale is structured; how hard and long you will have to work the business to recoup your investment; how anxious you are to purchase and how desperate the existing proprietor is to sell. You may find it useful to calculate estimates using different valuation approaches, make some subjective adjustments, and then discuss your estimates with your accountant. Before making a final decision, you might repeat the valuation process for several prospective businesses, increasing the probability of finding an excellent value.

One useful valuation approach may be called the *earning power method*. The approach involves a comparison of your personal earning power with that of the business.[6]

In other words, would you be financially better off (a) buying the business or (b) working for someone else and investing your money in financial instruments such as stocks or bonds?

STEP 1: Write down your estimate of the value of the business' assets. This might be an amount equal to that required to start a similar business yourself, less a fair amount for equipment depreciation, unusable inventory, bad debt write-offs, etc. The book value or whatever value the current owner reports may be greater or less than the actual value you estimate. Use your own estimate—to illustrate, we will use $300,000.

STEP 2: Calculate how much this amount would earn annually if invested elsewhere. For example, the stocks on the New York stock exchange have averaged a return of about 10% per year since the early 1960s. Therefore, an estimate of $30,000 ($300,000 x 10%) seems reasonable, although long-term diversified stock market investments are usually less risky than investing in a single small business.

STEP 3: Add your current annual salary—or what you could reasonably expect to earn working for someone else—to the $30,000, calculated in Step 2. ($35,000).

STEP 4: Compare the total ($65,000) to the business' projected annual profit ($90,000, for example). The excess of $25,000 ($90,000 minus $65,000) is the business' earning power.

Is the business' earning power adequate? If the business' earning power is less than zero, you should probably avoid buying the business. At least from a financial point of view, it would be

---

[6] A similar approach is recommended by the J.K. Lasser Tax Institute, in *How To Run a Small Business*, 6th edition, New York: McGraw-Hill, 1989.

more advantageous for you either to work for someone else, consider buying a different business, or create a new business as discussed in the next section.

If the business' earning power is greater than zero, as it is in our example, proceed to the next step by multiplying it ($25,000) by a subjectively determined factor ranging from 0 to 5. Zero (0) would be the factor used if there is absolutely no advantage to using the existing business' name, location, reputation, customer list or other aspects of the business you would inherit with the business that are included in Step 1. A factor of five (5) would correspond to a very reputable, well-established business with a strong growth potential that you probably would not be able to match easily by starting a new business. For our example, if the prospective business falls somewhere between the two extremes of zero and five—three, for example, multiply the previously computed $25,000 by 3. Add the resulting $75,000, to the asset base of $300,000 from Step 1.

Using the earning power method, our initial estimate of the business' value would be $375,000. This number may be adjusted to reflect additional considerations mentioned earlier. One additional consideration that could radically alter the transaction price is the structure of the sale. That is, how and when will the price be paid? For example, if the current owner agrees to a *seller carry* for all or a portion of the sale price—and I would be suspicious if s/he does not agree—what rate of financing is expected and how much of a security interest will be required? Obviously, a $375,000 sale financed at 10 percent would be more attractive to the buyer than the same $375,000 business financed at 12 percent. Other elements of the transaction's structure, such as valuation of specific assets and the timing of the closing, may have a significant impact on both your personal and business taxes, so make sure you work closely with a competent accountant.

CREATING A NEW BUSINESS

Most small business ventures begin with the identification of a key idea or concept. Eventually, the concept is parlayed into one or more core products or services that, ideally, offer unique benefits and advantages over the competition. The majority of these ideas arise in connection with the entrepreneur's previous work experience or personal interest. Other ideas stem from suggestions of friends, educational training or simply being in the right place at the right time.

A major pitfall to avoid is becoming so enthusiastic about the idea that you prevent yourself from *objectively* evaluating the idea's potential. It is easy to fall into such a trap when evaluating only one idea. That is why many large corporations initially screen a dozen or more ideas for every one new product they introduce. Consider the following three-step process to screen your business ideas.

STEP 1: Generate a number of new product/service ideas.

Reflect upon prior experiences and personal interests for new ideas, and brainstorm with friends and family. Read, read and read some more, staying alert to trends in business and society that may create new business opportunities. For example, consider some of the findings and implications of the volumes of 1990 U.S. census data available in most public libraries:

Total Population

Findings: The growth of the total U.S. population is slowing. The 9.8 percent growth witnessed in the 1980s is expected to be replaced by growth of only 7.0 percent in the 1990s.

Implications: Competition may intensify in many industries, with increased emphasis on retention of existing customers and qualified employees.

Regional Population Shifts

Findings: Large Southern and Western metropolitan areas experienced a much larger population growth rate (23 percent) than the rest of the country. Eight cities in Florida were among the twelve fastest growing.

Implication: These rapidly growing population centers are likely to represent the best locations for new businesses.

Household Size

Finding: The average household size dropped from 3.1 persons in 1970, to 2.8 in 1980, and to 2.6 in 1990.

Implications: The demand for smaller-sized, individual serving items is likely to increase, as is the popularity of businesses that are strong on interpersonal contact with customers—making customers feel the business is a home away from home.

Aging of America

Finding: The average citizen is about three years older than the average citizen was a decade ago.

Implications: The demand for products and services designed for older consumers is likely to increase. Simple things could make a big difference in a business' success, such as retail stores providing benches to allow easily fatigued elderly customers to sit periodically.

Atypical Households

Finding: The *traditional* family unit consisting of a married couple with children is disappearing, shrinking from 40 percent of all households in 1970 to only 26 percent in 1990.

Implications: Increasingly, businesses are becoming more sensitive to the needs of employees and customers who may be single parents.

Minority Involvement

Finding: The racial and ethnic mix of the population is becoming more diverse. While the population of whites grew by 6 percent in the 1980s, many minority groups grew at a much faster rate—13 percent blacks, 38 percent Indians, 53 percent Hispanics and 108 percent Asians.

Implications: Increasingly, in the 1990s businesses will become more sensitive to the needs and cultural differences of each group. Posted signs will become bilingual, more ethnic holidays will be recognized and supported, and there will be less tolerance toward racism against workers and customers.

In his book, *Starting A Home-Based Business,* Frederick H. Rice briefly describes over two-hundred business ideas that may be started on a small scale and run from your home. If you are contemplating your first business and hope to avoid a significant financial outlay, consider adding some of Rice's ideas to your list of possibilities. These include:

► Accounting or bookkeeping service

► Answering service

► Apartment rental service

► Appliance repair

► Aquarium service

► Auto cleaning and waxing

► Bakery

► Bargain shoppers' guide

► Bartering service

► Bed & breakfast

► Book exchange

► Budget counseling

► Bumper stickers

► Cake decorating

► Catering

► Chauffeur service

► Chimney sweeping service

► Cleaning service

► Collection service

► Computer operator

► Day care facility

► Dressmaker

► Farming

- Fence installation
- Floor refinishing
- Garage sales coordinator
- Game lessons
- Genealogy
- Home sitter
- Interior decorator
- Janitorial service
- Lawn care
- Messenger service
- Newsletter production
- Parking lot maintenance
- Pest control
- Pet motel
- Piano tuning
- Pool service
- Proofreading service
- Resume preparation service
- Secretarial service
- Security patrol service
- Telemarketing
- Travel agent
- Translator
- Welcome new neighbors
- Window and screen repair
- Window washing

Your Turn *Informational interviews are great ways to learn more about small business operations. Select one or more types of businesses you would like to consider further. Next, using a phone directory for a neighboring community, contact the owners of existing businesses. Arrange interviews to discuss what they like and don't like about owning their businesses, what their greatest challenges are, and so on. The information may help you decide which industries to enter, and which ones to avoid.*

STEP 2: Ask yourself tough questions about each idea.

These questions will help you to weed out losing ideas before you commit additional time and resources. Use the following questions to screen new product/service ideas. If you cannot answer these questions, you probably need to investigate further.

Question	Yes	Maybe	No	Not Relevant
Is there a genuine need for the product?	___	___	___	___
Is the need substantial enough to support a profitable business?	___	___	___	___
Do competitors currently offer similar products? If *yes,* does your idea offer distinctive advantages and customer benefits that competing products do not?	___	___	___	___
Is the product feasible to produce, and is the service feasible to deliver?	___	___	___	___
Is the product or service legal?	___	___	___	___
Is it safe?	___	___	___	___

Question	Yes	Maybe	No	Not Relevant
If the product is a durable good, can it be easily serviced? *Who* will service it?	——	——	——	——
Are the investment costs required to develop, produce and market the product reasonable and within your financial realities?	——	——	——	——
Is the *pay-back period*—the time necessary to recoup your investment—fast enough to allow you to stay in business?	——	——	——	——
Later, if the original is successful, can the product be expanded into a line of similar or compatible items?	——	——	——	——
Can you protect the product with a patent or copyright?	——	——	——	——
Does the product infringe upon anyone else's patent or copyright?	——	——	——	——
Are needed raw materials and supplies readily available?	——	——	——	——

STEP 3: Conduct some exploratory research to test the waters.

Many entrepreneurs have failed because they could not confidently answer the questions in Step 2. Others have failed because they were so convinced of the soundness of their business idea that they completely bypassed the opinions and reactions of key people other than themselves—namely industry experts, suppliers, middlemen and, most importantly, end users or consumers. In both instances, exploratory research could effectively further screen ideas and increase the likelihood of selecting the ideas with the greatest potential.

The following popular and relatively inexpensive techniques are commonly used in exploratory research:

Literature surveys and secondary data (also known as "rummaging around in the library"). The voluminous nature of reference material and secondary data (i.e., data already collected for another purpose, such as the census data previously mentioned) that can be found in the library is spectacular. Books, periodicals, journals, government documents and other sources in the library address the following types of issues for each business idea:

Statistical information

> ► Characteristics of competitors
> ► Industry trends (e.g., revenues)
> ► Consumer characteristics—demographic and otherwise
> ► Characteristics of suppliers
> ► Economic activity and buying power of counties and *standard metropolitan areas* (SMAs)

Qualitative information

> ► Identification of industry leaders, experts or trade associations who may be able to provide additional information
> ► Identification of potential suppliers
> ► Current issues facing the industry and ideas pertaining to the future of the industry
> ► Information pertaining to why other businesses in the industry have been successful or have failed
> ► Current industry practices
> ► Identification of technical *how to* information (e.g., how to develop a blueprint to accompany a patent application)

The key advantages to data and information found in libraries are low cost, ease of access and speed of attaining it. Some of the material, such as industry statistics, may not be available elsewhere. On the downside, the data is sometimes out of date or may not fit your needs precisely.

In searching for information about specific industries, you will probably find it useful to familiarize yourself with Standard Industrial Classification (SIC) codes. Learning SIC codes will help you locate specific information about the industry you are considering entering. In addition, if your new business' customers will be other businesses, as opposed to household consumers, knowledge of the SIC codes will help you gather information to understand their needs.

The classification system, published in the *SIC Manual* by the Office of Management and Budget, assigns numerical codes to each type of business. Codes with the first two digits ranging from 19 to 39, for example, correspond to manufacturing businesses, while 70 to 89 correspond to service businesses. Subsequent digits in the code place each business into smaller and better defined industry categories. Several government publications, such as the *Census of Business* and non-government reference sources such as the *F & S Index*, are organized by SIC codes. If you know the SIC code, you will be able to locate specific industry information quickly. Here are a few examples of SIC codes:

SIC Code	Industry
286	Industrial organic chemicals
2992	Lubricating oils and grease
3291	Abrasive products
3541	Screw machine products
3622	Industrial controls
3679	Electronic components
7231	Hair stylists
7363	Temporary help services
7538	Auto repair, general

SIC Code	Industry
7933	Bowling centers
8021	Dentists
8051	Nursing homes

Experience surveys. This informal technique involves picking the brains of industry experts and potential future business associates who hold differing viewpoints and perspectives. If a new product is the core of your business idea, for example, query the following people:

► Engineers (e.g., can the product be effectively and efficiently designed?)

► Suppliers (e.g., are the necessary materials, component parts and manufacturing equipment readily available at a reasonable price?)

► Middlemen (e.g., would retailers be receptive to carrying the product?)

► Marketing consultants (e.g., how should the product be positioned in the consumer's mind relative to competing products?)

► Employment agencies (e.g., is the labor market adequate to support your new business? That is, how difficult will it be to find qualified job applicants?)

► Government officials (e.g., are there any licensing, safety or environmental requirements of which you should be aware? Will warning labels or disclaimers be required?)

► Competitors (e.g., how are they doing? What changes have they made in product design, pricing, distribution, etc.?)

► Former manufacturers of similar products (e.g., why do they no longer manufacture the product?)

► Union leaders (e.g., what are their perspectives of the challenges facing the industry?)

Focus groups. To solicit initial consumer reactions to your business ideas, conduct a series of informal discussions with groups of six to eight prospective customers. Properly structured, focus groups can provide vital information pertaining to consumer preferences and purchasing habits. Often, these discussions generate mountains of data, since one consumer's comment will prompt another group member to speak, which sparks another comment from a third person, and so on. Be cautious when you interpret the groups' comments; consumers are often more enthusiastic in focus groups than they are when making purchasing decisions.

Following are a few issues and questions you might use to guide focus group discussions. Be aware that the *personality* of each focus group is different, which often leads to comments in one group that differ quite a bit from those generated in another.

- Describe the *typical* purchaser of the proposed product, or typical patron of the proposed store, etc.

- Why might someone *not* be interested in the product?

- If the product were not available in one store, would the typical consumer settle for a substitute, or would s/he search for the product in another store? Answers to this question will give you a feel for who the strongest competitors might be.

- How many units would the typical consumer purchase? How frequently?

- Describe the possible uses of the product.

- What would be a reasonable price for such a product?

- What do you like and dislike about similar competing products—or alternatives—that are currently on the market?

- Who in the household would make the purchase decision? Who would use it? Who would make the actual purchase? Who would influence the decision?

- How should the item be packaged (e.g., individually, by the dozen)?

- What color(s) should the product be? What size? What special features (e.g., a handle)?

- Where would you expect to be able to buy such a product (e.g., at a department store, specialty store, convenience store, through direct mail)?

After you complete the initial screening process, you may need to conduct more conclusive research to accurately estimate the technical and marketing feasibility of the most promising business ideas. This research might include, for example, substantial prototype development, as well as formal surveys, test markets and panel usage tests. This research can be quite expensive; in most cases it should not be undertaken until your business idea has successfully survived the exploratory research stage.

A creative combination of research techniques might also be used. For example, a few years ago I was called upon to help launch a new company that would manufacture technical devices to help industrial engineers measure the level of toxic substances known as PCBs. The manufacturer had only a vague notion of which types of businesses might be prospective customers. We did some exploratory research, placing an ad in a general trade magazine. The ad offered additional information upon request and asked interested businesses to supply their address and SIC code. We used this information to determine which industries and geographic regions would be most receptive to the new device. We then designed a detailed survey to gather additional specific information from prospective customers in these target groups.

Once you have done the preliminary screening of your new business possibilities, you are ready to prepare a more detailed business plan. Chapters three through fourteen outline the small business planning process.

ASK YOURSELF

► What are the advantages and disadvantages of each of the three primary ways of owning a business—buying a franchise, buying an existing business and creating a new business?

► Of the three alternatives, which option is most appealing to you? Why?

GEARING UP TO PREPARE YOUR BUSINESS PLAN

WHY PLAN?

"If you don't know where you're going, any path will take you there."

— Theodore Levitt

After reading the first two chapters, you are probably convinced that the world of small business is not something to be entered haphazardly. To increase the probability of business success, you must do your homework. Your homework began when you screened franchise opportunities, existing businesses and ideas for new businesses to identify the winning candidates. The next step in your homework process is to prepare a written business plan.

A business plan is a carefully prepared document that outlines the nature of the small business, the objectives of the entrepreneur, and the proposed actions that will enable the entrepreneur to reach those objectives. The business plan is analogous to a roadmap; it should guide you through a maze of business decisions and alternatives filled with twists, turns, sidestreets and dead ends.

Although not every entrepreneur formally prepares a business plan before starting his or her business, the advantages of doing so far outweigh the disadvantages. The process of preparing a business plan stimulates thought. It requires the entrepreneur to think strategically and to explicitly articulate and face critical issues that might otherwise be ignored or postponed.

To illustrate, a few years ago a U.S. manufacturer stumbled across what appeared at the time to be a great opportunity. He decided to build a manufacturing plant in a small rural community in South America. His *plan* was to manufacture the goods at that location and truck the finished product to a port city several miles away. From there, the goods would be shipped around the world. After investing heavily to build the plant, the entrepreneur learned that the primitive roads between the plant and the port would not support the weight of the trucks required to transport the manufactured goods. He realized, too late, that additional planning might have helped to avoid such a mishap.

Another reason to prepare a business plan is that a plan facilitates greater coordination and integration of efforts than would be possible if the business were simply operated on a day-to-day basis. For example, a part of a well designed plan will outline the job roles of each key employee. This ensures that all employees understand the scope of their responsibilities and how their individual jobs contribute to the overall success of the enterprise.

A well written plan helps the entrepreneur communicate with others (i.e., partners, employees, investors). It clearly articulates the vision and expectations for the business. By seeing the vision presented clearly, these individuals are more likely to understand it, embrace it and work toward making it a reality. In short, a plan will improve the odds of everyone working as a team.

A thorough, concise and persuasive plan convinces lenders and investors that the entrepreneur is serious about starting a business. It demonstrates that he has done his homework. Few financial backers seriously consider any plan that is not written. Writing a plan increases the likelihood that the business venture will be adequately funded.

Finally, consider the benefits of a written plan serving as a reference document. It can be used to measure progress toward business goals, and as a foundation for future planning. If the stated objectives of one plan are not met, corrective actions can be incorporated into the next plan. In this way, planning becomes a circular process; reviewing one plan creates a springboard for the next plan.

AVOID EXCUSES

Despite the advantages of preparing a written business plan, some hopeful entrepreneurs bypass the process. They rely upon informal, vague and implicit plans that either prevent the start-up or ultimately limit the effectiveness of the business. If you are reluctant to prepare a formal written plan, you may wish to reconsider your position after reading the following reasons that are sometimes used to avoid writing a plan.

Time Pressures

If your excuse is that you do not have time to prepare a plan, how will you find time to operate your business after the start-up? The first business plan you ever write may seem like an overwhelming, time-consuming task; like most tasks, the process becomes quicker with experience. Remember that planning done properly *saves* time.

Fear of Failure

Planning involves specifying goals and objectives. If you are reluctant to commit your goals and objectives to paper where others may see them, maybe you are afraid peers and associates will say "I told you so" if your business fails. If that is the case, you may not be thick-skinned enough to start your own business. Besides, if you do not articulate your goals, how will you know when you have reached them?

Limited Understanding of the Business, Industry or Customer

Planning is difficult when you lack knowledge. Goals, strategies and operational decisions become fuzzy. It is impossible to commit fuzziness to paper in a meaningful way. If your base of knowledge is insufficient, the initial analysis of your business idea may have been inadequate. If so, you would be wise to temporarily postpone preparation of your plan until you collect more information.

Poor Writing Skills

Much of your plan's preparation involves you sitting at a desk or table and writing, rewriting and revising your plan. This may be mentally tiring and time consuming if your previous experience has not included much writing. Writing is a basic form of communication, with which all businesspeople should feel comfortable; consider using the plan as an opportunity to polish your writing skills. Consider hiring a professional proofreader to read the final document. Many universities and community colleges have "writing labs", where trained professionals are available to assist those who ask.[7]

Low Self-Confidence

Preparing a plan implies that the businessperson who writes it controls the implementation and accomplishment of the plan. Understandably, there may be some reluctance to plan when the would-be planner believes the destiny of the business is randomly determined. Rarely, however, does sheer luck determine the fate of business. If specific risks or uncertainties could affect the success of the business, disclose them in the plan. For example, if your goal is to open a ski resort, demand for your service may be affected by weather conditions, which are obviously beyond your control.

STEPS IN THE SMALL BUSINESS PLANNING PROCESS

Before committing the business plan to paper, think through the planning process analytically. That is, gather data needed to prepare the plan, identify factors that could influence successful implementation of your plan, choose between alternative courses of action, bombard yourself with "what if . . . ?" questions, anticipate results and formulate contingency plans.

The planning process involves a continuous sequence of eight interrelated steps, illustrated on the adjacent page, in *The Planning Process for Small Business*.

Step 1, a *situation analysis*, is essentially an assessment of the status quo. What do prospective customers like or dislike about currently available products? Who are likely competitors?

---

[7] For two excellent books on business writing, order *Better Business Writing* and *Writing Fitness* from the back of this book.

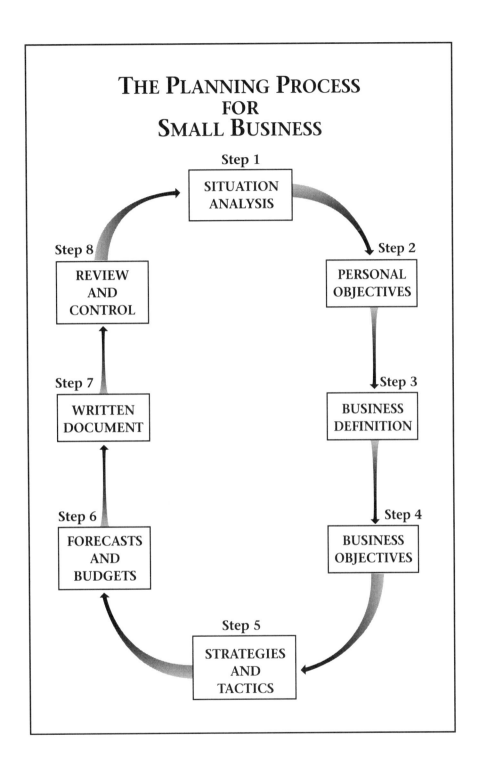

THE PLANNING PROCESS
FOR
SMALL BUSINESS

Step 1
SITUATION ANALYSIS

Step 2
PERSONAL OBJECTIVES

Step 3
BUSINESS DEFINITION

Step 4
BUSINESS OBJECTIVES

Step 5
STRATEGIES AND TACTICS

Step 6
FORECASTS AND BUDGETS

Step 7
WRITTEN DOCUMENT

Step 8
REVIEW AND CONTROL

Your Turn

Contact a local university that offers one or more courses in entrepreneurship and small business. Ask the professors who teach these courses to allow you to read some plans developed by their students as term projects. Not every professor will cooperate, and not every student's plan will be worth reading, but you may stumble across some useful information as well as a few great ideas to help you to organize and present the information you gather for your plan. Other than the time it takes to make a few phone calls and read a few papers, there's nothing to lose.

Step 2 is to identify your personal objectives. Why do you *really* want to own your own business? What do you expect from the business? How much time, money and energy are you willing to invest?

Defining your business is the third step in the planning process. Who is the customer you would like to appeal to? What customer needs will your business satisfy? How will your business satisfy those needs?

In Step 4 you will articulate your objectives for the business. How many units would you like to sell during your first year of operation? How many customers will you plan to serve? How profitable should the business be?

Step 5, formulating strategies and tactics, is one of the more detailed and time consuming steps. Here, decisions involve how the business will achieve the objectives you outlined in Step 4. What prices will you charge? What will the manufacturing process entail? How will you train your employees?

Step 6 is forecasting and budgeting. Given the level of resources committed to the business, what level of sales should materialize during your first year in the operation? During the second year? During the third year? At these sales levels, what should your expenses be for raw materials, labor, overhead, etc.?

The written document is Step 7, which combines all the decisions and estimates you identified in the first six steps, clearly organized for future reference.

In Step 8 you will review the written document and take corrective actions. In this review and control step, the planner asks: Were my stated objectives achieved? If not, why not? What actions are appropriate to improve my business' future performance?

Chapters four through fourteen examine the steps in the small business planning process in greater detail.

ASK YOURSELF

▶ How do business plans help improve the chances of entre-preneurial success?

▶ Are you a good planner? Why or why not? What can you do to improve your planning skills?

▶ What are the steps in the planning process for small business? How are the steps related to one another?

CHAPTER
FOUR

CONDUCTING THE SITUATION ANALYSIS

CHAPTER FOUR

YOUR FIRST STEP

Your first step in planning a small business is to conduct a situation analysis. This involves carefully reviewing the environment in which your small business will compete. In other words, what potential problems, opportunities, threats, trends and other relevant issues are likely to influence your business' success and the selection of your business strategies?

THE PLANNING PROCESS FOR SMALL BUSINESS

Your situation analysis should scrutinize the market in terms of customer characteristics and the nature of the customer-product relationship. A careful evaluation of specific competitors can also be quite revealing, as can a comprehensive review of alternative communities and specific sites where the business might be located.

The four checklists that follow may be useful in systematizing your analysis. You may find that you have already collected much of the needed information during the earlier process of screening business ideas.

Customer/Product Analysis

Ask the following questions for each major product group and for each major customer segment. Do not *just* ask the questions: find the answers, investigate past trends and likely future trends, and carefully consider the implications.

- ► Who is the likely customer?
  - Where does s/he live?
  - Where does s/he work?
  - What is his/her age?
  - What is his/her income?
  - What is his/her level of education?
  - What is his/her sex?
  - What is his/her family composition?
  - Is he/she mobile?

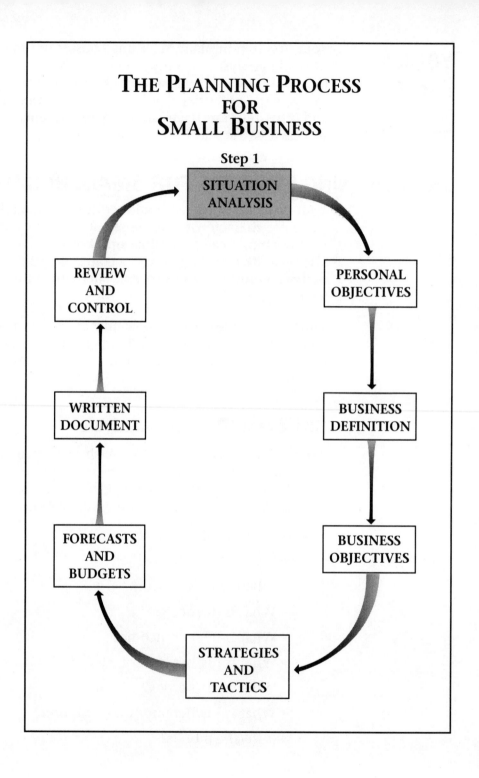

THE PLANNING PROCESS FOR SMALL BUSINESS

Step 1

SITUATION ANALYSIS

PERSONAL OBJECTIVES

REVIEW AND CONTROL

WRITTEN DOCUMENT

BUSINESS DEFINITION

FORECASTS AND BUDGETS

BUSINESS OBJECTIVES

STRATEGIES AND TACTICS

- What is his/her lifestyle?
- What are his/her social and religious beliefs?
- If the likely customers are other businesses:
  - What is their size?
  - What are their industry's sales potential?
  - What are their SIC codes?
  - Who are their customers?
  - What are their purchasing procedures?

► How many likely customers are there?

► What are customers' quality expectations?

► Are customers likely to perceive a purchase risk?

► Is purchase inertia likely to be a problem?

► What needs does the product satisfy? Think carefully about this question.

► How is the product used?

► Are there alternative uses?

► Is the product a necessary or discretionary purchase?

► How often is the product purchased by the customer?

► How many units is the customer likely to buy?

► Might the product cause storage problems for the customer?

► How often will the customer buy?

► When will the customer buy (day of the week, time of day, season of year, etc.)?

► Is the product a convenience good or a shopping good?

► If the product is a service, does the customer need to be present when the service is provided?

► Where would the customer learn about the product (e.g., through friends, business associates, TV advertising, yellow pages)?

► Who *actually buys* the product (e.g., Mom, Purchasing agent)?

- Who *influences the decision* to buy? (e.g., kids, engineers)?

- Why should the customer buy your product and not the competitor's?

- How much prior knowledge does the customer have about the product (i.e., is it truly a new innovation)?

- How much would the customer likely pay for the product?

- How sensitive would s/he likely be to price changes?

Checklist for Evaluating The Community

This checklist is useful when evaluating alternative communities for small businesses that will ultimately depend on the community in which they are located. Retail stores, consumer service businesses, small manufacturing and distribution businesses are examples of businesses that are often community-dependent. Avoid selecting a community solely because you live there. Instead, carefully consider the following questions:

- Is sufficient labor available?
- How much competition is there among local businesses for qualified and/or trainable employees?
- What are the prevailing wage rates?
- How many local high school and college graduates are available? How many leave the area after graduation?
- Is the area highly unionized?

Are suitable sites available?

- Are they economically affordable?
- Are they accessible to traffic?
- Are they accessible to modes of transportation appropriate for your type of business?
- Are there opportunities to lease as well as to purchase?

What is the economic base of the community?

- What are the dominant industries?
- How diversified is the local economy?

► Are adequate financial and credit facilities available?

► How is the economic base expected to evolve over the years?

Are adequate sources of supply available?

► How many? Are they competitive?

► Are they reliable?

► What are their costs for delivery?

► How much order lead time do they require?

► What services do they provide?

Are there adequate TV stations, newspapers, radio stations, etc.?

► What are their ad rates?

► What additional services do local media provide?

What about the population?

► What is the population size of the community?

► How many residents own their own homes?

► How affluent is the community?

► What are the relevant past and future trends? For example, is the community growing? If so, in what direction?

What local regulations or ordinances might influence your business' operation?

► What is the tax burden?

► What are the zoning requirements?

► What about the blue laws?

► Are there special licensing laws for your type of business?

► Can you, your customers and your employees tolerate local smoking laws or lack thereof?

Would *you* like to live there?

► Are neighborhoods neat and clean?

► Are streets, parks and public areas safe, well maintained and pleasant?

►Are adequate schools, utilities, health care and other professional services, recreation alternatives, churches, etc., available?

►Can you tolerate the climate?

►Are fire and police protection adequate?

Are there other considerations?

►Is housing available for your future employees?

►Would the climate help or hurt your business?

►Do nearby communities or metropolitan areas *steal* a disproportionate number of consumers from the area?

►What is the general attitude toward business?

►Are energy costs reasonable?

Checklist for Evaluating Specific Sites

After you have selected a community or neighborhood for your new business, use the following list of questions to evaluate specific sites. The importance or weight of each factor will depend largely upon the size of your operation, as well as the type of business. For instance, availability of customer parking usually will be a more critical consideration for retailers than for manufacturers.

► What is the total cost to acquire or lease the property? What is the acquisition cost per square foot?

► What is the total estimated cost for necessary repairs, remodeling and renovation? What about special heating, lighting or ventilation requirements? What are these costs per square foot?

► Does the site provide as much space as you need, including parking and the possibility of later expansion?

► Will customers visit your place of business—as opposed to a business that might call on customers or operate through the mail? If so:

• Is adequate, convenient and safe parking available?

• Is public transportation available?

- Is the location likely to generate drop-in or impulse consumer traffic?

- Is the site conveniently located near the customers' residences or businesses? If not, will savings in acquisition costs offset the cost of the customers' inconvenience?

- Is the site located on a main street or artery, or in an otherwise familiar area (e.g., a mall)? If not, will savings in acquisition costs offset the increased advertising and promotion costs required to inform customers of your location?

▶ What are the zoning regulations for the site and for the surrounding area?

▶ What other types of businesses are located in the area? Are they compatible with your type of business?

▶ Are there several vacancies in the area? If so, why?

▶ What is the crime rate for the immediate area?

▶ Is crime insurance available? Is it affordable?

▶ What fire and police protection is available?

▶ Are adequate utilities available at a reasonable cost (e.g., water, electricity, sewer, gas)?

▶ If snow is likely, are snow removal services available? Is the site located along a high priority *snow route*, or on a side street that may not be plowed at all?

▶ Will you pick up and/or deliver merchandise? If so, is the site located near expressways or major arteries, to minimize driving time?

▶ If the site is for rent or lease, what are the terms of the rental agreement? Consider length of lease, renewal option, penalties for breaking the lease, services provided by the landlord, maintenance or other fees, etc.

▶ What is the history of the site? That is, what types of businesses previously occupied the site? Why are they no longer there?

Analysis of Competition

Use this checklist to evaluate the competitors your business is likely to face. Be careful not to define your competition too narrowly. For example, if you are considering opening a movie theater, your competition is not limited solely to other movie theaters. Rather, you will be competing with VCR rentals, mini-golf courses, bowling centers and other forms of entertainment vying for consumers' discretionary dollars.

► Who are your potential competitors?

► What are their strengths?

► What are their weaknesses?

► Who are the customers of each competitor?

► Why might a consumer buy from them instead of you?

► What is the sales level for each competitor? Are there significant trends in sales?

► What is the market share of each competitor?

► What is the cost structure of each competitor?

► What is the pricing structure of each competitor?

► Do competitors enjoy a strong consumer franchise? That is, how loyal are each competitor's customers?

► How do competitors promote their products and businesses?

► What is the distribution structure of each competitor?

► Who are the suppliers of each competitor?

► What are the objectives of each competitor?

► How is each competitor positioned? That is, what is the mental image that comes to the consumer's mind when s/he thinks of each competitor?

► Are there potential future competitors not currently operating in the industry? If so, who?

► What are the capabilities of each competitor's proprietor(s), manager(s) and employees?

- ► Are the competitors well financed?
- ► How committed is each competitor? That is, have competitors invested so much in their businesses that they will be forced to vigorously compete after you enter the market?
- ► Are future technological developments likely to alter each competitor's product line and/or mode of operation?
- ► How does each competitor's product line rate, in terms of breadth and depth?
- ► How do competing products rate in terms of quality, size, appearance, durability, packaging, etc.?
- ► What are the credit granting practices of each competitor?
- ► Do competitors *stand behind* their products? That is, how do their warranties rate?
- ► What sort of auxiliary services do competitors offer (e.g., gift wrapping, installation, delivery, maintenance and repair)? Are customers charged separately for these services?
- ► Do competitors own any patents or exclusive distribution *rights* that would affect your market entry?
- ► If competitors are retail stores or service businesses, how do their physical facilities rate in terms of layout, decor, cleanliness, parking, convenience of location, ambiance, etc?
- ► What are their hours of operation?
- ► Within the community, how saturated is the competition? In other words, is there room for your new business?

ASK YOURSELF

► What are the key elements of a situation analysis?

► What might be the consequences of neglecting each aspect of the situation analysis?

CHARTING YOUR COURSE: ESTABLISHING OBJECTIVES AND DEFINING YOUR BUSINESS

<table>
<tr><td>

A CLOSER LOOK

</td><td>

In this chapter, we take a closer look at Steps 2, 3 and 4 in the small business planning process—articulating your personal objectives, defining the business and determining the business' initial objectives.

</td></tr>
</table>

ARTICULATE YOUR PERSONAL OBJECTIVES

Owning and operating your own business requires commitment and self-motivation. Commitment and self-motivation must be directed toward some objective, purpose or rationale. If you have trouble articulating why you want to go into business, you may have trouble channeling your energies later. Or, you may find yourself going into business for the wrong reasons or with unrealistic expectations. The realities of long hours, hard work and ultimate responsibilities of owning a business will quickly discourage the uncommitted entrepreneur who has not thoughtfully assessed the demands of this major decision.

When identifying personal objectives, you have several questions to consider. First, are you primarily interested in wealth, security, self-esteem, achievement, power or social affiliation? Your personal objectives will influence your business objectives. A working couple, for example, may not feel an overpowering need for supplemental income, but may have a strong desire to interact with other people. They might opt to establish a small retail store with only modest income potential, with a tremendous potential for one-on-one personal interaction with customers.

Second, how much risk are you willing to assume? In most manufacturing industries and some service industries, the profit potential per unit is much greater if the size of the business' capacity is expanded. In operating a bowling center, for example, a center with forty lanes costs *considerably less* than twice as much to build and operate than does a center with only twenty lanes. Therefore, upside profit potential may be several times higher for the larger bowling center; of course, there is greater downside risk in that those profits can be real-

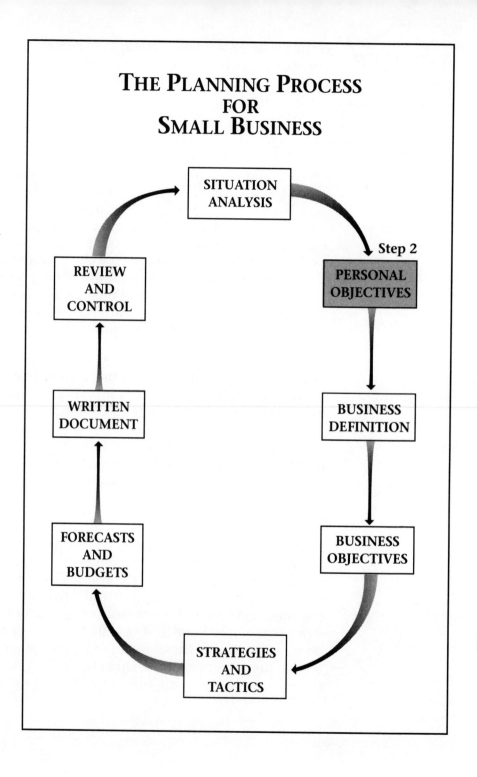

THE PLANNING PROCESS FOR SMALL BUSINESS

SITUATION ANALYSIS

Step 2

PERSONAL OBJECTIVES

REVIEW AND CONTROL

BUSINESS DEFINITION

WRITTEN DOCUMENT

BUSINESS OBJECTIVES

FORECASTS AND BUDGETS

STRATEGIES AND TACTICS

ized only if the demand for bowling is high enough to keep all forty lanes occupied.

Another question to consider is: How long and hard are you willing to work? Most businesses require some level of sustained commitment before becoming profitable. Avoid thinking that you will only have to work hard for a few months to get the business established. Instead, think in terms of the level of commitment you are prepared to make for at least three to five years. Remember that your business is not your only activity sphere. Develop a personal policy to help balance your role as an entrepreneur with your roles as a spouse, parent, citizen, church member, etc.

Next, consider what is a reasonable timetable for your objectives. That is, what do you want your business to do for you in the first year of operation? Second year? Third year? etc.

Fifth, how will you know if you have reached your objectives? Ideally, objectives should be clearly stated, unambiguous and quantified. For example, rather that having an objective such as "making as much money as I can," plan for a specific amount of money such as "$40,000 in the business' first twelve months of operation."

Sixth, will you be able to survive if you fail to meet one or more of your objectives? Are you prepared to pump most of the business' initial earnings back into the business? Even though the business may be profitable, it may require more cash than it is able to generate to finance its growth.

Finally, if your business is not as profitable as you would like, how will you know when it is time to get out of business? I remember one enthusiastic individual who opened his own retail store. After almost a year of trying to stimulate demand he still had very few customers. But because he had become so emotionally attached to the business, he could not bear to close it until he was almost bankrupt.

DEFINE THE BUSINESS

This step in the planning process involves answering a seemingly obvious and elementary-type question: What business will you be in? By now, you probably know what sort of business you are planning, but it is helpful to clearly delineate what you envision your business is or is not. Otherwise your business may take on a life of its own—with no clear direction of where it is going and no integrated effort to get it there.

Your Turn

To better understand business definition statements, write to several publicly-owned businesses in the industry you have decided to enter. Ask for copies of their annual reports—which may also be available at a nearby public library. Scrutinize the business definitions or "mission statements" published in these documents to see what they have in common. The similarities may relate to the factors needed to successfully operate a business in that industry.

Ideally, try to define your business on the basis of the customers you plan to serve and the type of goods and services you plan to offer. No business that fails to satisfy customer needs can survive. Yet, it is largely a business' goods and services that distinguish it from competitors and gives rise to consumer choice, so a product dimension is also relevant. When defining the business, consider three key questions:

1. **WHO** is the customer? Refer to the customer description developed when you conducted the *Situation Analysis*. If competitors are well entrenched, it may be wise to identify smaller market niches that the competition has ignored.

2. **WHAT** customer needs will be satisfied by the business? Needs may be broadly categorized as primary (viscerogenic: e.g., need for food, water, warmth) or secondary (psychogenic: e.g., need for achievement, social affiliation, knowledge, power, self-esteem). If properly engineered and positioned in the consumer's mind, most products are capable of satisfying several needs simultaneously.

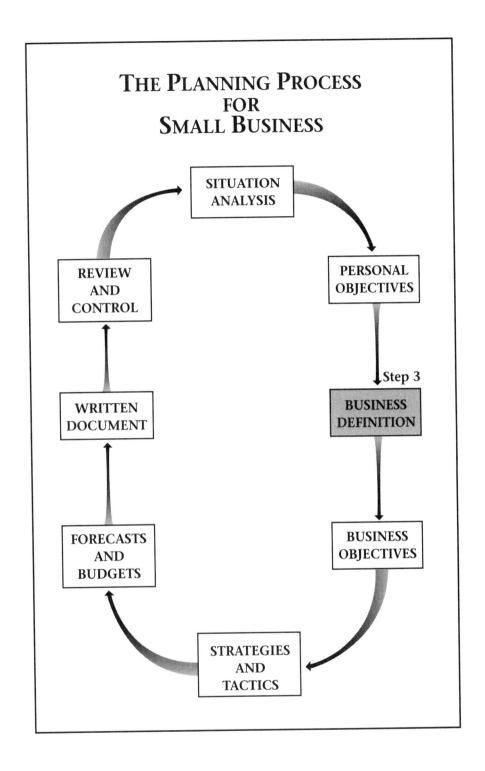

THE PLANNING PROCESS
FOR
SMALL BUSINESS

SITUATION
ANALYSIS

REVIEW
AND
CONTROL

PERSONAL
OBJECTIVES

Step 3

BUSINESS
DEFINITION

WRITTEN
DOCUMENT

FORECASTS
AND
BUDGETS

BUSINESS
OBJECTIVES

STRATEGIES
AND
TACTICS

3. **HOW** will the business satisfy customer needs? With what goods? What services? What technologies? What processes?

When defining the business, be careful not to be too narrow or too broad. Too narrow a focus may myopically ignore potential opportunities—and competitors. Too broad a focus may fail to provide direction for the business. Notice that possible answers to the *who*, *what* and *how* questions below range from very specific to very broad.

1. **WHO** is the customer?

Examples: Young children with a sweet tooth. Hungry individuals who want a snack. All consumers.

2. **WHAT** customer needs will be satisfied?

Examples: Need for glucose. Need to quickly quench hunger in a pleasant fashion. Need for enjoyment.

3. **HOW** will the business satisfy customer needs?

Examples: Manufacture candy bars. Provide good-tasting snacks. Provide consumers with food products.

Based upon the above examples, an appropriate business definition might be as follows:

Business Definition: We will manufacture and market good-tasting snacks to enable individuals to quickly satisfy their hunger.

IDENTIFYING BUSINESS OBJECTIVES

Businesses do not become successful by accident. Rather, the entrepreneur must establish objectives for the business. *Objectives* should be measurable and attainable benchmarks for goals. *Objectives* are usually expressed in terms of survival, growth, profitability or revenues. For example, a business' *goal* may be "to maximize profitability," whereas the corresponding *objective* might be "to attain a 12 percent return on net worth for the initial year of operations." Such an objective is specific enough that the entrepreneur can continuously evaluate the business'

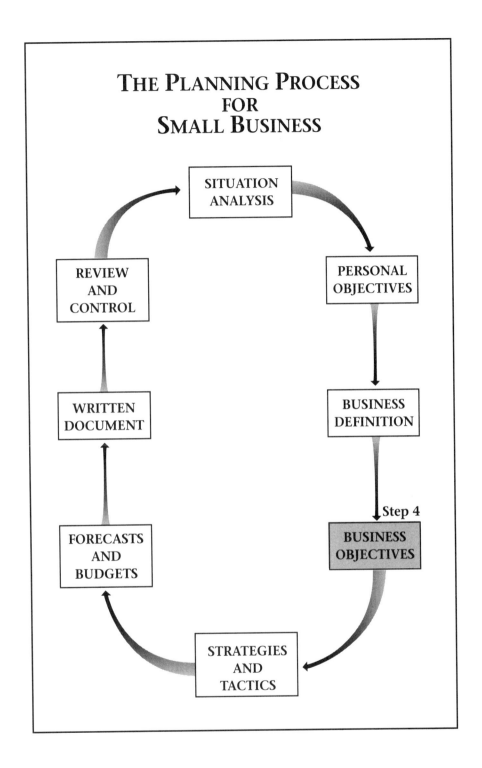

THE PLANNING PROCESS
FOR
SMALL BUSINESS

SITUATION
ANALYSIS

PERSONAL
OBJECTIVES

REVIEW
AND
CONTROL

BUSINESS
DEFINITION

WRITTEN
DOCUMENT

Step 4

BUSINESS
OBJECTIVES

FORECASTS
AND
BUDGETS

STRATEGIES
AND
TACTICS

progress, and can take corrective action as necessary. To avoid stating objectives and monitoring progress toward them is analogous to playing a basketball game in total darkness. The players may be able to hear the ball hit the backboard, but no one knows the score, no one knows which team is winning, and no one knows whether adjustments in either team's strategy are appropriate.

A business' definition and goals may remain fairly stable over a long period of time. However, a business' objectives are likely to vary from period to period. This reflects changes in the environment and changes in the business' competitive posture. For example, maximizing profitability may always be a key goal, but a downward adjustment in profit objectives might be appropriate during a recession.

Following are several examples of possible objectives. It is probably useful to initially focus on only a few. Notice the characteristics of well-stated objectives, which tend to be:

▶ *Quantitative.* Most are expressed in precise numerical terms, although some objectives are inescapably qualitative.

▶ *Time-frame specific.* To specify a time frame for an objective is to hold yourself accountable.

▶ *Flexible.* If the business environment changes radically, you should not feel badly about adjusting the level of the objectives or the time frames for their accomplishment.

▶ *Understandable.* If they are not clear to you and your employees, you may have trouble reaching them.

▶ *Realistic.* Be honest with yourself and with the potential investors you may eventually attempt to woo with your plan.

▶ *Consistent.* Avoid multiple objectives that may be contradictory (e.g., "build market share" vs. "increase profitability per average order").

Types of Business Objectives and Selected Examples

Sales Objectives (e.g., totals by product, by customer segment, etc.)

Dollar sales growth

Unit sales growth

Market Share

Number of new accounts

Average order size

Examples: "Sell 1,000 units of product A and 500 units of product B by December 31, 1993."
"Maintain a minimum market share of 3 percent of all carbonated beverage sales in the state of Texas during 1993."

Financial Objectives

Return on Net Worth (RONW)

Return on Sales (ROS)

Return on Assets (ROA)

Net Worth

Inventory turnover

Accounts receivable

Working capital

Examples: "Attain an overall ROS of at least 2 percent for 1990."
"Do not allow total accounts receivable to exceed more than 25 percent of net sales for any monthly period during the first three years of operation."

Other Objectives

New equipment and processes

New plants

New offices

Geographic expansion

New product introductions

Product quality

Customer complaints

Business image

Examples: "Begin producing all of our own products by February 28, 1989."

"Beginning in September 1988, resolve to the satisfaction of the customer, 95 percent of all monthly complaints, within five business days."

While considering your business' definition and goals, it is appropriate to ask, "How *high* a RONW should I shoot for?" "What is an appropriate *level* of sales for my business?" "How *many* times should my inventory turn over?" etc. Unfortunately, there are no easy answers. The appropriate level of each objective depends upon a number of factors, such as:

► Market potential

► Access to capital

► Type of business (e.g., manufacturing, retail, service)

► Strengths and weaknesses of the business

► Nature and extensiveness of competition

► The owner's aggressiveness and willingness to assume risk

► The financial structure of the business (e.g., proportion of debt financing vs. equity financing)

► The cost structure of the business' products

► Likely economic and industry trends

There are at least four general tools or approaches to utilize when setting business objectives. These include: 1) references to your personal objectives; 2) norms for the business—if already established—or industry; 3) break-even analysis; and 4) the strategic profit model.

Personal Objectives

These will provide some direction to help you decide how ambitious your business objectives should be, how much risk the business should assume, and what level of profitability the business should achieve.

Business or Industry Norms

If you are buying an established business, study past financial statements to learn how the business has performed historically. These statements are most useful when formulating revenue, cost of goods, overhead expenses and profitability objectives. Examine enough historical data to identify apparent trends, e.g., are sales increasing annually or are they stable? Ideally, three to five years of data are needed to assess these trends. Performance indicators, such as the number of customers and market share, tend to be more subjectively estimated, so the business' past records may be less helpful when establishing some objectives.

Once the business' past performance and trends have been identified, consider how your expertise, vision and plan for the business will influence them. Then, adjust the past performance indicators to reflect realistic future performance.

If you are building a new business, you might refer to performance statistics published by companies such as Dun and Bradstreet, Robert Morris and Associates, and industry-specific trade associations. These organizations publish several financial ratios and other statistics for a number of companies and industries. Much of this information is available in public libraries. Be careful when evaluating industry-wide data, however; these statistics aggregate the performances of poorly managed and struggling businesses with those of successful businesses.

Break-even Analysis

Successful entrepreneurs are able to quickly assess the relationship between their costs, revenues and profitability. If you can estimate your costs and have an idea of the level of profitability you want to achieve, break-even analysis can help you determine an appropriate sales goal. For example, suppose you estimate the following:

$5,000 = monthly fixed or direct costs (e.g., rent, salaries, insurance, other overhead)

$30 = average sale price of each unit

$10 = per unit variable cost of producing each unit

$2,500 = desired level of monthly profitability

Your break-even point (BEP) or minimum number of monthly unit sales necessary to cover costs and desired profitability would be computed as follows:

$$BEP = \frac{\$5{,}000 + 2{,}500}{30 - 10} = 375 \text{ units}$$

Note that the BEP calculation also helps to quantify the degree of risk that might be involved in alternative business strategies. For example, we might extend the above analysis to consider the consequences of investing an extra $1,000 per month in a new technology that would enable us to produce each unit more cheaply—say $8 each. Then, our BEP calculation becomes:

$$BEP = \frac{\$6{,}000 + 2{,}500}{30 - 8} = 386 \text{ units}$$

Under this scenario, the BEP increases slightly. We would have to sell eleven more units before reaching our profit objective. However, any additional unit of sales beyond 386 will generate a gross profit of $22 (i.e., $30 – $8); whereas, if we decide not to invest in the new technology, each additional sale will generate a gross profit of only $20 (i.e., $30 – $10). Remember, there is not necessarily a *right* choice. Investing $1,000 in the equipment increases the risk level, because it pushes up the BEP. Profitability will increase *if* sales exceed 386 units, but so will the losses if sales fall below 386 units.

Strategic Profit Model

A key long-term objective of most small businesses involves return on net worth (RONW)—i.e., net profit after taxes, expressed as a percentage of the business' funds invested by the proprietor(s). As a primary measure of profitability, however, RONW is influenced by a number of intervening determinants. This includes the rate of return on the total assets of the business and the degree of business leverage. In turn, these are influenced by other considerations as shown in *The Strategic Profit Model*[8], which follows.

The point is that there are many different ways to impact RONW. Once you have set a target objective for RONW, the strategic profit model can be useful in establishing a consistent set of objectives for the numerous components of RONW. Similarly, the model is also useful in understanding how a slight change in one variable, such as net sales may ultimately influence RONW. If net sales decrease by 10 percent, for example, RONW may decrease by more or less than 10 percent.

---

[8] Source: *Modern Retailing: Theory and Practice* 5th ed. By J. Barry Mason and Morris L. Mayer, Plano, TX: Business Publications, Inc. 1990, page 312.

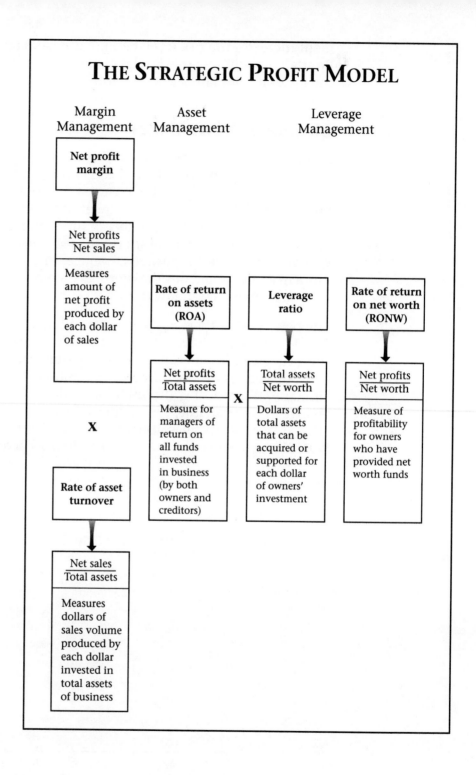

THE STRATEGIC PROFIT MODEL

Margin Management	Asset Management	Leverage Management

Net profit margin

$$\frac{\text{Net profits}}{\text{Net sales}}$$

Measures amount of net profit produced by each dollar of sales

X

Rate of asset turnover

$$\frac{\text{Net sales}}{\text{Total assets}}$$

Measures dollars of sales volume produced by each dollar invested in total assets of business

Rate of return on assets (ROA)

$$\frac{\text{Net profits}}{\text{Total assets}}$$

Measure for managers of return on all funds invested in business (by both owners and creditors)

X

Leverage ratio

$$\frac{\text{Total assets}}{\text{Net worth}}$$

Dollars of total assets that can be acquired or supported for each dollar of owners' investment

Rate of return on net worth (RONW)

$$\frac{\text{Net profits}}{\text{Net worth}}$$

Measure of profitability for owners who have provided net worth funds

ASK YOURSELF

▶ What are your personal objectives for your own business?

▶ How will your business affect your personal life?

▶ What will happen to you, your family, and your business if you fail to meet your objectives? How will you feel? How will you react?

▶ What immediate objectives do you have for your new business?

▶ What vision do you have for your new business? How will you describe it in five years? Ten years? Twenty years?

CHAPTER SIX

HAMMERING OUT STRATEGIES AND TACTICS: ORGANIZATIONAL CONSIDERATIONS

STRATEGIES AND TACTICS

"Strategy is the company's concept of how to win the war. Tactics are derived activities designed to win battles."

— Philip Kotler

When you identify business objectives as described in the previous chapter, you establish benchmarks for your business' performance. Your next step is to develop specific courses of action to enable your business to reach those objectives. Broadly speaking, these courses of action entail both strategies and tactics. Although this chapter and the five that follow generally examine strategies and tactics simultaneously, Kotler's message refers to the distinction between the two:

▶ **STRATEGIES** are the *major* courses of action the business utilizes to pursue its objectives.

▶ **TACTICS** are the *secondary* courses of action that help to support or implement the strategies.

If, for example, sales growth is the key objective of your business, then part of your growth strategy might be to add additional products to your existing product line. One appropriate tactic might be to hire a Research and Development consultant to systematically solicit and screen ideas for new products.

The initial objective a budding entrepreneur usually faces is to get the business opened to begin operations. Consequently, most of the critical early organizational and operational decisions are a combination of strategic and tactical choices that involve at least seven different operational areas:

▶ Organization

▶ Production

▶ Personnel

▶ Marketing

▶ Purchasing and Inventory Control

▶ Record keeping

▶ Insurance

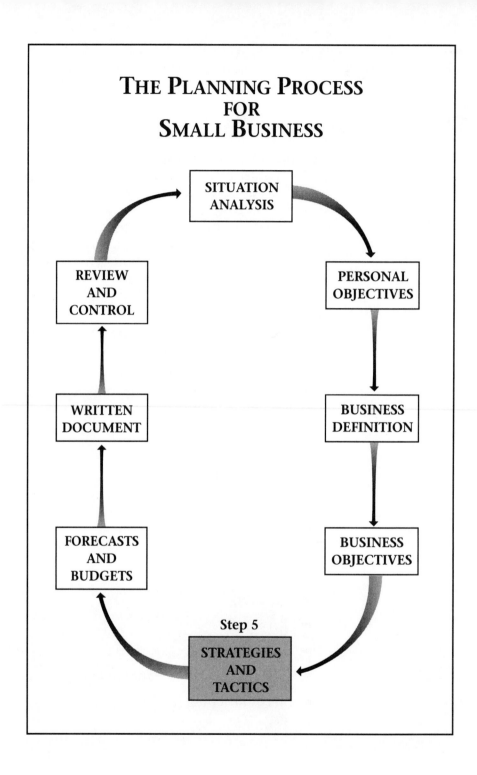

THE PLANNING PROCESS FOR SMALL BUSINESS

SITUATION ANALYSIS

PERSONAL OBJECTIVES

REVIEW AND CONTROL

BUSINESS DEFINITION

WRITTEN DOCUMENT

BUSINESS OBJECTIVES

FORECASTS AND BUDGETS

Step 5

STRATEGIES AND TACTICS

We will take a closer look at each of these decision categories by first examining the organizational choices, which involve issues of legal structure, organizational design and business exit.

LEGAL STRUCTURE

Before you begin operating a business, you must decide on the legal structure of your business—that is, will it be a sole proprietorship, a partnership or a corporation? The appropriate form of your organization will depend upon a number of factors. You may want to solicit the advice of an attorney and an accountant in your state before you make a final determination. Antonio M. Olmi of the Small Business Administration recommends that budding entrepreneurs investigate eight specific questions when choosing a legal structure:

1. What is the size of the risk? That is, what is the investors' liability for debts and taxes?

2. What would the continuity (life) of the firm be if something happened to the principal or principals?

3. What legal structure would insure the greatest adaptability of administration for the firm?

4. What is the influence of applicable laws?

5. What are the possibilities of attracting additional capital?

6. What are the needs for, and possibilities of, attracting additional expertise?

7. What are the start-up costs and procedures?

8. What is the ultimate goal and purpose of the enterprise? Which legal structure can best serve its purpose?

The advantages and disadvantages of each form of legal structure are outlined on the next page (see *Alternative Legal Structures*). A related consideration that may affect your options is whether to become a franchisee or not, as discussed in Chapter 2. That is, the legal structure of the franchise may be contractually determined by the agreement with the franchisor.

Alternative Legal Structures[9]

Sole Proprietorships (i.e., business is owned by only one person)

Advantages

- Ease of formation
- Sole ownership of profits
- Control and decision-making vested in one owner
- Flexibility
- Relative freedom from government control and special taxation

Disadvantages

- Unlimited liability
- Unstable business life (e.g., if owner should die)
- Ordinarily, less available capital than in other types of business organizations
- Relatively difficult to obtain long-term financing
- Relatively limited viewpoint and experience of proprietor

Partnerships (i.e., business is owned by two or more persons)

Advantages

- Ease of formation
- Direct rewards
- Growth and performance facilitated
- Flexibility
- Relatively free from government and special taxation

Disadvantages

- Unlimited liability of at least one partner
- Unstable life of business (e.g., if one partner should die)

---

[9] Source: *Selecting the Legal Structure of Your Firm,* Antonio M. Olmi, U.S. Small Business Administration, Management Aid #6.004, 1985.

- Relatively difficult to obtain large sums of capital

- Firmly bound by the acts of just one partner as agent

- Difficulty of disposing of partnership interest (e.g., if one partner wants to buy out the other partner)

Corporations (i.e., a legal entity distinct from those parties or individuals that own it)

Advantages

- A stockholder's liability limited to fixed investment amount

- Ownership readily transferable

- Separate legal existence

- Stable and relatively permanent existence

- Relatively easy to secure capital in large amounts and from many investors

- Can draw on expertise and skills of more than one individual

Disadvantages

- Activities limited by corporation's charter and by various laws

- Manipulation by minority stockholder possible

- Extensive government regulations and required local, state and federal reports

- Less incentive if manager does not share in profits

- Expense of forming a corporation

- Double taxation (i.e., income tax on corporate net income and on individual salary and dividends, although this can be avoided by selecting a *Subchapter S status*

In addition to these three garden variety choices of sole proprietorship, partnership and corporation, there are at least two more possibilities. You may want to consult a local attorney to explore them. The *Subchapter S status* corporation has a big advantage since it bypasses the double taxation dilemma. At least six states (Wyoming, Colorado, Florida, Kansas, Virginia and Utah) offer another option, the *Limited Liability Company* (LLC) which avoids double taxation and offers other attractive advantages.

THE ORGANIZATIONAL CHART

Another organizational concern is the way responsibility and work assignments will be divided in your business. If you have no partners, no employees and no consultants, the answer is simple: you will do everything yourself. But, if the business will be more than a one person operation, you will have to select a form of organizational structure to make sure the business runs smoothly.

The form of organizational structure you select will affect the way your staff works together, and how efficiently and effectively tasks are performed. A useful exercise is to design an organizational chart such as those shown on the following pages. Note that, as the business changes through the years, so may the appropriateness of each design. It is not uncommon to periodically redesign the organizational chart, although frequent changes may create somewhat chaotic transition periods, which can result in morale problems among employees, as well as other problems.

Examples of Organizational Charts

LINE ORGANIZATION

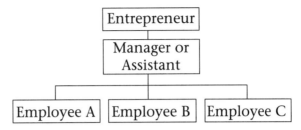

Appropriate when: Jobs are simple and routine; few employees; entrepreneur can stay in complete control.

FUNCTIONAL ORGANIZATION

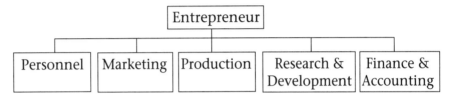

Appropriate when: Need for efficiency is important; several employees; fairly stable business environment.

GEOGRAPHIC ORGANIZATION

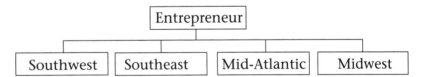

Appropriate when: Business operations are geographically dispersed; customer preferences and/or competition vary from one area to the next.

PRODUCT SPECIALIZATION

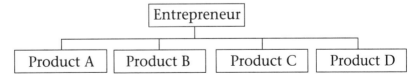

Appropriate when: Business offers several unrelated products.

CUSTOMER ORGANIZATION

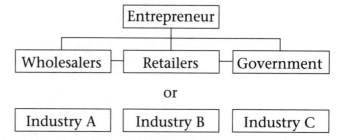

Appropriate when: Needs and appeals vary from one customer group to the next.

Your Turn

If you are currently employed, find a copy of your workplace's organizational chart. As practice, redesign it to improve the overall efficiency and effectiveness of the operation. Next, consider how the work routine would be affected (e.g., which employees might receive marching orders from different supervisors) and the extent to which some employees might resist the new organizational structure.

BUSINESS EXIT AND SUCCESSION PLANNING

In their zeal to launch their businesses, entrepreneurs may plan start-up organizations; few develop contingency plans for later reorganizations and *what ifs*. Consider the following questions that might be relevant to your new business:

▶ In a partnership, what will happen to the business if one of the partners suddenly becomes ill, disabled, dies, retires or simply loses interest in the business and wants out? Who will assume the partner's duties in the business? How will that person be compensated? Will the leaving partner or his heirs have any rights to assets, copyrights, patents or future profits? How will these values be determined? Are partners obligated to buy one another's share of the business? If so, under what circumstances? How will the proceeds of the business be divided if the business is sold?

► Similarly, in a sole proprietorship, what happens to the business if you suddenly die? As founder, does your will address who should run the business and how business assets or earnings should be distributed to beneficiaries? If you divorce, what claims will your spouse have on assets and future earnings of the business?

► If you plan to pass the business on to another family member or to someone else, when and how will the transition be handled? How will the sale price be determined? Will you have any role in the business after ownership is passed?

Of course, it is impossible to anticipate and plan for every possible twist of fate the future might hold. Some forethought can help avoid bitter dissagreements between partners, burdensome courtroom battles, excessive taxes, family disputes and other hardships. For example, a recent study by the Chicago Economic Development Commission found that the jobs of approximately 15,000 manufacturing workers in Chicago are in jeopardy because the proprietors of these small businesses are over 55 years old and have no plans for succession.

With the help of an attorney and an accountant, draw up a buy-sell agreement, establish a trust or estate freeze, revise your will, or try some combination of these. At the very least, talk with partners and other relevant parties, and try to reach a consensus and commit the agreement to paper. Then, periodically review the document to keep it current.

ASK YOURSELF

▶ Which form of legal structure appeals to you? Why? What are the disadvantages or risks of this legal structure?

▶ Describe the type of business that might be best suited for each of the five types of organizations discussed in the chapter.

▶ What would you like to see happen to your business in case you should suddenly die after you begin operations?

CHAPTER
SEVEN

PRODUCTION
DECISIONS

DECIDE BEFORE YOU START

Production decisions involve the processes by which tangible goods are manufactured and intangible services are provided. These decisions play a key role in the overall business strategy because product quality, cash flow, control, costs and continuity of supply are all affected by the production alternatives you select.

Several production decisions should be contemplated prior to starting-up your business. These include whether you will manufacture or purchase component parts and resale items, how much production capacity you will create, what raw materials and equipment you will need, how the production or service process will be established, how much space your business needs, and what levels of product/service quality you will seek.

MAKE OR BUY

Will you manufacture or purchase tangible goods? It may be tempting to believe that manufacturing all component parts or resale items yourself will save money, but this is not always true. Consider the technical expertise, quality and dependability of other potential manufacturers. Also consider the initial fixed costs required to produce the product yourself—including space, equipment, training of workers, and materials inventories. Finally, consider the value of maintaining control over proprietary processes or ingredients. You will not want to share your trade secrets with another manufacturer who may become your competitor.

A practical alternative during start-up might be to purchase from other manufacturers; then, perhaps later, you will produce the items yourself. Or, consider purchasing major component parts or sub-assemblies from other manufacturers and doing the final assembly yourself. If you are uncertain whether you should *make or buy*, examine the remaining production decisions you will need to make, should you ultimately decide to do the manufacturing yourself.

CAPACITY CONSIDERATIONS

What capacity level do you desire? That is, how many items would you like to be able to produce in your production operation? This decision will impact the amount of physical space you need, as well as the number of employees and quality of equipment you require. High-capacity operations often enjoy economies of scale, but have higher fixed costs that may take years to recoup. Conversely, low-capacity operations tend to have higher variable costs, but lower fixed costs and greater flexibility of production.

RAW MATERIALS AND EQUIPMENT

What raw materials, equipment and supplies will you need in the manufacturing process? Are they readily available at a reasonable price? Can you lease or purchase the equipment? It is advisable to contact potential suppliers before beginning operation. Suppliers often make useful suggestions that aid in the planning process. These issues will be considered further in Chapter 10.

FLOWCHARTING

What operations will you require in the production process? What is the sequence of those operations? How much time will you need for each? Could you combine, eliminate, accelerate or sub-contract some operations? These considerations will impact the layout of your plant, the space you need, the number of employees you need, the skills you need, and when you schedule production runs. Developing a production operations *flow chart* for each item manufactured, as illustrated on the next page, can be a useful example.

You can use the same flow chart technique in a service operation, to outline the process by which the service is performed. With a service flow chart, the critical points when customers interact with employees can be identified and used to improve the quality of those interactions.

Finally, keep in mind that production operations, equipment and facilities must comply with the Occupational Safety and Health Act of 1970. Write to the U.S Government Printing Office for a copy of *Standards for General Industry*.

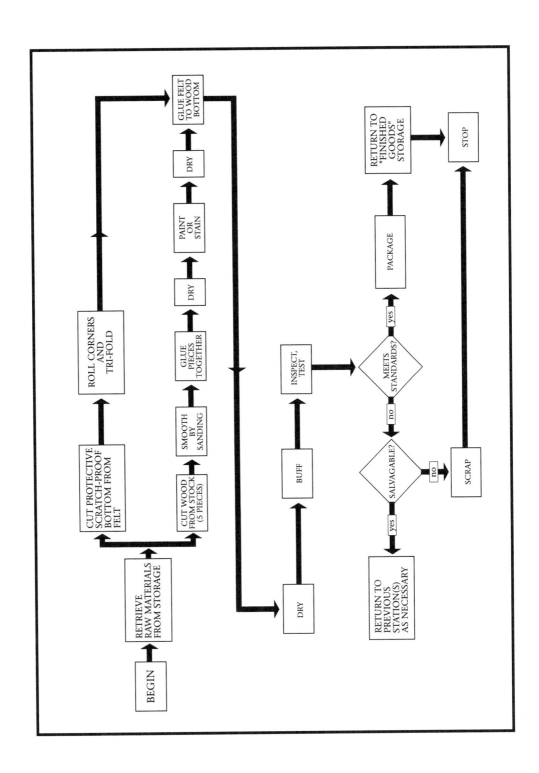

Your Turn

Practice flow charting for a service business by charting your experience the next time you dine out. The first step might be an encounter with a sign that instructs you in some way (e.g., "Please wait to be seated.") Interactions with employees should be noted especially, as well as where the encounters took place, how much time elapsed during each encounter, and what tasks were performed by employees during each encounter.

Note that in many service businesses, such as restaurants, the customer himself plays an important role in "producing" the service. In this sense, customers become quasi-employees who have to learn their roles and responsibilities before they can be served and satisfied. For example, as a customer you might be expected to create your own salad, signal the waiter, specify how you would like the food prepared, bus your own table, etc. How customers perceive their service "jobs" influence whether or not they return, so the flow chart for a service business should not ignore the role of the customer.

SPACE

How much space will you need? In addition to the plant facilities, previously alluded to, you will want to plan space necessary for storing raw materials, supplies, tools, component parts and finished goods. Also consider additional space for restrooms, employee lunch areas, employee/visitor parking, delivery loading and unloading, an office, and possible future expansion.

QUALITY

"The improvement of quality in products and the improvement of quality in service—these are national priorities as never before."

President George Bush

What level of quality do you desire? How will you measure quality? How will you maintain consistent quality? Who will be responsible for delivering quality? Entrepreneurs often assume that high quality standards are expensive and that customers will be unwilling to pay for quality. While these concerns are sometimes justified, in the long run it is often more expensive to sacrifice quality. Inadequate quality creates dissatisfied customers who may take their patronage elsewhere and be costly to replace. Unhappy customers may return defective merchandise for expensive repair or replacement, tell their friends and family not to buy your "shoddy products," or complain to the retailer who may stop ordering from you.

The Malcolm Baldrige National Quality Award

Recognizing the importance of quality to the national economy, in 1987 Congress passed Public Law 100-107, which created the Malcolm Baldrige National Quality Award. The award recognizes U.S. businesses that have made great strides in manufacturing and service quality. The prestigious award is bestowed upon no more than six businesses each year—up to two manufacturers, two service businesses and two small businesses. IBM Rochester, Xerox Business Products, GM Cadillac, Motorola and Federal Express are some of the most recognizable companies among the elite that have won the award.

Since the first winner was announced in 1988, interest in the award has gained momentum. In 1991, for example, more than 200,000 requests for the award application were made. Although only a small number of businesses that request the guidelines apply for the award, the informative 40-page booklet that accompanies the application promises to assist any quality-conscious entrepreneur who reads it. For example, here are a few of the key principles of quality offered by the team of experts who administer the award:

► Genuine quality is defined by the customer, not by the entrepreneur.

► The entrepreneur and top managers need to create clear quality values and build the values into the way the business operates.

► Quality excellence derives from well-designed and well-executed systems and processes.

- ► Continuous improvement must be a part of the management of all systems and processes.

- ► Companies need to develop goals, as well as strategic and operational plans to achieve quality leadership.

- ► Shortening the response time of all operations and processes of the company needs to be part of the quality improvement effort.

- ► Operations and decisions of the company need to be based upon facts and data.

- ► All employees must be suitably trained and developed, and involved in quality activities.

- ► Design quality and defect and error prevention should be major elements of the quality system.

- ► Companies need to communicate quality requirements to suppliers, and work to elevate supplier quality performance.

Bonus Offer!

To receive a *free* copy of the guide to establishing a quality improvement program in your business, contact the National Institute of Standards and Technology, Route 270 and Quince Orchard Road, Administration Building, Room A537, Gaithersburg, Maryland 20899. Or call them at (301) 975-2036. Ask for a copy of the application guidelines for the Malcolm Baldrige National Quality Award. This information is also available to businesses headquartered outside the U.S., although they cannot formally apply for the award.

ASK YOURSELF

▶ What are the risks involved in manufacturing your own products? What are the risks of *not* manufacturing them?

▶ Do you have the expertise to establish your own production operation? If not, where can you acquire additional information?

▶ Why is quality such a critical competitive issue in the 1990s?

STAFFING THE BUSINESS: HUMAN RESOURCES

BUILDING YOUR TEAM

Unless your planned business will be extremely small and you will do all of the work, consider how you will build a competent team of employees and supervisors to make the business function. The time you invest in developing a *human resources* plan is well spent, because few entrepreneurs can make the business succeed without the help of knowledgeable and enthusiastic employees. Without them, product quality, employee productivity and customer service suffer.

Most strategic and tactical staffing decisions for small businesses revolve around five key questions:

1. What type of employees do you need?

2. How many employees do you need?

3. How should potential employees be recruited and screened?

4. How should employees be trained?

5. How should employees be compensated and motivated?

Evaluation of each employee's job performance is another consideration, though not of immediate concern when you are opening the business.

CONDUCTING JOB ANALYSES

To determine the type and number of employees you need, conduct a series of *job analyses*—one for each job. That is, think through the requirements of each employee's job and how productive each employee should be after an initial training and orientation period. Experts in the industry or industry trade associations may be able to help. Some job tasks may be grouped together so that employees performing those tasks need not be as highly skilled, or as highly paid, as employees who will perform other tasks. Organizing jobs in this fashion could reduce the business' payroll costs and increase work efficiency. On the other hand, it could also limit employee scheduling flexibility, and customer service might suffer.

Job Descriptions

Upon completion of each job analysis, write job descriptions and job specifications for each job. A *job description* is a formal, written statement that describes the nature of the specific job, its requirements and its responsibilities. Job descriptions are useful tools for planning work to be done. They also guide the rest of the staffing process. They help match jobs to applicant qualifications and create expectations for applicants who are eventually hired.

It is not uncommon for small businesses that do not have clearly defined and written job descriptions to end up with employees who define their jobs in the context of their most preferred job tasks. These favorite activities may not be the same set of tasks the proprietor had in mind for them. A sample job description on the following page.

Job Specifications

A *job specification* is a statement that converts the job description into people qualifications—that is, the abilities, skills, level of education and experience necessary for an employee to perform successfully in the specific job. An example of a job specification follows this description.

When preparing a job specification, avoid the temptation to set the qualifications too high. Doing so may discourage some motivated, qualified individuals from applying. And, once hired, *over*qualified applicants may become bored with the job.

Also, avoid stating job specifications in a way that might unfairly—and illegally—discriminate against applicants on the basis of gender, race, religion, ethnic origin or other factors that have nothing to do with one's ability to perform the job. For example, if a job will require heavy lifting, do not specify that the applicant should be a male, based on a belief that men can lift more weight than women. You cannot assume that *every* prospective male applicant will have the strength to do the job, or that *every* prospective female applicant will *not* have the needed strength. Instead of specifying *male*, list only the strength requirements.

Sample Job Description

POSITION TITLE: SNACK BAR ATTENDANT[10]

Purpose: To sell, prepare and serve food and beverages to customers.

Duties:

1. Prepare food according to established methods and portions.

2. Operate cash register and complete food checks, where applicable.

3. Maintain immaculate cleanliness of all snack bar areas and ensure hygienic conditions.

4. Maintain refrigerator, freezer and inventories in an orderly and clean manner.

5. Clear and clean tables.

6. Set tables, where applicable.

7. Clean and fill napkin and condiment containers.

8. Requisition and receive food and supplies, where applicable.

9. Arrange display of food on back counter, where applicable.

10. Adhere to Board of Health regulations.

11. Insure Alcoholic Beverage Commission regulations are honored.

12. Clean entire snack bar area at end of shift.

13. Other duties as assigned.

Directs Work Of: (Not applicable)

Responsibility: This position is responsible for specific routine assignments under direct supervision.

---

10 Source: Bowling Center Job Descriptions, Arlington, TX: The Bowling Proprietors Association of America.

Sample Job Specification

POSITION TITLE: SNACK BAR ATTENDANT[11]

Education: Eighth Grade

Experience: Experience of six months in food and beverage service preferred. If required to handle alcoholic beverages, see local regulations regarding age.

Knowledge: Able to operate a cash register. Basic knowledge of food and beverage preparation procedures.

Judgment: Minimal use of judgment is required because the duties to be performed are based on established procedures and direct instruction. Problems are referred to a higher level for solution.

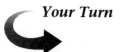

Your Turn

Evaluate the job description and job specification for the last job you held. How might the documents be improved? Try rewriting or updating them for practice.

DEVELOPING AND SCREENING THE APPLICANT POOL

After preparing job descriptions and specifications, prepare a strategy to generate a pool of applicants. As a general rule-of-thumb, generate four reasonably qualified applicants for each position. This will increase the likelihood of hiring well qualified individuals. Classified advertisements, employment agencies, college placement offices, trade associations, trade journals and word-of-mouth advertising are potential sources for generating a pool of job applicants. Once you open your business on-premise advertising may also be used to encourage customers, employees and visitors to spread the news of job vacancies.

Of course, not every applicant will be qualified. Fortunately, there are several ways to detect and screen out unqualified applicants. Depending upon the job requirements and qualifications demanded, consider using some combination of appli-

---

[11] Source: Bowling Center Job Descriptions, Arlington, TX: The Bowling Proprietors Association of America.

cation blanks, resumes, employment references, interviews, employment tests and honesty tests.

Application Blanks

Application blanks provide an initial and inexpensive way to quickly screen for applicants who are clearly not qualified. Applications can be structured to emphasize key job qualifications determined in the job analysis. Professionally developed, standardized application blanks may be obtained at most office supply stores. Consider using one of these initially. Later, after you have learned what information is most critical in determining which applicants are likely to be successful in each job and which applicants are unlikely to be successful, you can design your own form.

Resumes

These popular tools represent an alternative to application blanks. Their organization may vary from applicant to applicant, so it may be difficult to objectively compare and contrast potential employees.

Employment References

Employment references indicate applicants' *intangible* qualities (e.g., responsibility, punctuality, demeanor, work attitudes and ability to work with others). Fearing litigation, many employers will hesitate to speak negatively about former employees; you may have to listen to what references do not say, as well as to what they do say. One useful *bottom line* question is to ask the former employer: "Would you hire this person again?"

Personal Interviews

Interviews are useful in assessing applicants' interpersonal communication skills. For example, does the applicant speak clearly? Are his or her comments thoughtful, well organized and understandable? Does the applicant listen attentively? Are effective nonverbal communication skills such as smiling and eye contact apparent? These skills are especially important if the job involves working on a regular basis with customers, employees or other people.

Unfortunately, it is difficult to objectively evaluate other skills in the interview process. However, there are several questions that you may ask to understand an applicant's employment expectations, level of enthusiasm, job interests and career ambitions. The following list includes some of the questions you might ask during the interview.

Three Dozen Useful Job Interview Questions[12]

1. What are your long-range and short-range goals and objectives? When and why did you establish these goals? How are you preparing yourself to achieve them?

2. What specific goals, other than those related to your occupation, have you established for yourself for the next ten years?

3. What do you see yourself doing five years from now?

4. What do you *really* want to do in life?

5. What are your long-range career objectives?

6. How do you plan to achieve your career goals?

7. How much do you expect to be earning in five years?

8. Why did you choose the career for which you are preparing?

9. Which is more important to you, the money or the type of job?

10. What do you consider to be your greatest strengths and weaknesses?

11. How would you describe yourself?

12. How do you think a friend who knows you well would describe you?

13. What motivates you to put forth your greatest effort?

14. How has your education prepared you to work for me?

15. Why should I hire you?

16. What qualifications do you have that make you think that you will be successful in my business?

---

[12] Source: Adapted from materials supplied by the College Placement Office, West Texas State University, Canyon, TX.

17. How do you determine or evaluate success?

18. What do you think it would take to be successful in a business like mine?

19. In what ways do you think you can make a contribution to this business?

20. Do you have plans to continue your education?

21. Do you think that your grades are a good indication of your academic achievement?

22. What have you learned from participating in extra-curricular activities?

23. In what kind of work environment are you most comfort-able?

24. How do you work under pressure?

25. In what previous jobs have you been most interested? Why?

26. What two or three things are most important to you in your job?

27. Are you seeking employment in a company of certain size? Why?

28. What criteria are you using to evaluate the company for which you hope to work?

29. Do you have a geographical preference? Why?

30. Describe the relationship that should exist between a supervisor and those reporting to him or her.

31. What two or three accomplishments have given you the most satisfaction? Why?

32. Why did you decide to seek a position with this business?

33. Are you willing to travel?

34. Are you willing to spend at least X months as a trainee?

35. What major problem have you encountered? How did you deal with it?

36. What have you learned from your mistakes?

There are also questions you should avoid in the interview. These relate to issues of unfair discrimination that may seem like harmless chit-chat to you, but may subject you to a lawsuit if an applicant you turn down believes that he or she was denied the job because of irrelevant questions you asked in the interview. For example, questions regarding age, marital status, religion and intentions to marry, retire or have a baby are definitely taboo.

Employment Tests

These tests may be used to assess an applicant's aptitude, personality, knowledge, skills and interests. Professionally developed, *pre-packaged* tests are recommended because their validity usually has been established already. In other words, valid tests have previously demonstrated statistically that they measure what they purport to measure. Detailed information regarding employment tests is available from local employment agencies and testing centers.

Honesty Tests

An alarming number of job applicants are not completely truthful on application blanks or in job interviews. For example, one study found that 45 percent of applicants had overstated their responsibilities on a previous job. Other estimates suggest that dishonest employees steal at least $5 billion worth of money, merchandise and supplies from U.S. businesses each year. Honesty tests can help to screen out these undesirable applicants.

In many states, the popularity of polygraph honesty exams (i.e., lie detector tests) has given way to paper and pencil honesty exams. These tests are often more convenient, less expensive and legally less restrictive than the polygraph. By analyzing the patterns of responses to a series of tough questions, paper and pencil test developers can assess the likelihood of an applicant engaging in dishonest job behavior if he or she is hired. Here is one such question:

Suppose a father of ten children worked at a retail store for fourteen years. He was paid monthly, but was always short of cash by the middle of the month. So he often took $20 to $30 from the cash register during the middle of the month to buy food for his children. After being paid, however, he would always return the money to the register. One day the store owner found out what the employee had been doing and fired him. Do you believe the owner made the right decision? Why or why not?

TRAINING

Once you select and hire an employee, you will need to provide training on the job. Training might involve on-the-job experience, working side by side with you or with previously trained employees. An effective training program might also utilize a combination of any of the following methods:

- ▶ Lectures
- ▶ Discussions
- ▶ Policies and procedures manual
- ▶ Demonstrations
- ▶ Videotapes
- ▶ Case analyses
- ▶ Role playing
- ▶ Self-study books

Customer-contact employees such as receptionists, retail sales clerks, waiters and other workers who will interact with customers should be trained on at least two dimensions. The *technical* dimension includes job tasks such as familiarization with paperwork, equipment operation, and product knowledge. While the technical dimension focuses upon *what* the employee does for the customer, the *personal* dimension focuses upon *how* the employee does it. Prompt service, thanking the customer, smiling, empathetically listening to and resolving customer complaints, and offering assistance proactively to customers are a few of the many pertinent issues categorized along the personal dimension. In today's marketplace, failing to address and train in both dimensions may mean handing competitors a substantial competitive edge.

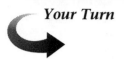

Your Turn   *To learn more about commercial training materials that are currently available, browse through training-related trade journals at your local public library. Contact some of the advertisers in these magazines for more information about the training tools they offer.*

COMPENSATING THE WORK FORCE

You will compete for top notch employees, just as your business will compete for good customers. Your ability to pay competitive wages will affect the quality of your employees. Keep in mind, however, that the total costs of compensation packages often exceed direct wages by as much as forty percent, when you include:

▶ Employer's contribution to social security

▶ Unemployment compensation

▶ Workman's compensation/disability

▶ Sick leave, vacations, holidays

▶ Major medical and/or life insurance

▶ Pension contributions

▶ Retirement plans

▶ Profit-sharing, bonus agreements or deferred compensation plans

Also consider that substantial labor costs may stem from recruiting, hiring, training and replacing employees—as well as the possible costs of employee mistakes, accidents and theft.

When designing your compensation program, consider the motivational potential of the *method* of pay vs. the *level* of pay. A sales employee, for example, may be more motivated if she is paid a $6 commission per unit sold with a sales quota of 500 units, than if she were paid a straight salary of $3,000. Other financial incentives can also be motivational (e.g., sales contests), as are many non-financial programs such as recoginition and praise, employee-of-the-month awards, challenging work assignments, promise of promotion, and daily contact with employees.

ASK YOURSELF

▶ How many employees will you need in your new business?

▶ What tasks will employees in your business perform?

▶ What skills and other qualifications will employees need to do their jobs?

▶ Where will you find qualified applicants?

▶ How will employees be trained, compensated and motivated?

CHAPTER NINE

MARKETING: MORE THAN SELLING

SATISFY YOUR CUSTOMERS

"A customer is the only thing an entrepreneur can't survive without."

Phillips Goodell

Marketing involves the exchange of valued goods and services for money or for other considerations. Properly done, both the business and customers benefit. The business generates revenues to cover its costs, expenses and profits, while customers receive satisfaction from quality products and services that meet their needs.

The long term success of any business requires that the entrepreneur be as concerned with the customers' perspectives as s/he is with the business'. That is, it is in the best interest of the business and the entrepreneur to make sure that customers are satisfied—that the business has the right products that customers want, not simply what the business wants to sell; that customers get what they pay for; that the products perform; that the business honors both explicit and implicit promises to customers; and that customer complaints are promptly, courteously and satisfactorily addressed. The role of marketing in today's competitive marketplace embraces much more than advertising and selling.

By paying careful attention to satisfying customers, the business also benefits. For example, customers are more likely to continue to do business with companies that satisfy them than with those that do not. Continued patronage can be very profitable. One study found that the typical service business loses about 20 percent of its customers each year. When the attrition rate can be cut to 15 percent, profits jump an incredible 25 to 85 percent![13]

These increased profits result from a number of factors. First, it usually costs much less to service an existing customer than to attract and establish an account for a new customer, replacing one that was lost. Second, long-standing customers tend to spend more with the business than newer customers. And third, satisfied customers tell their friends and family about the business, which is free advertising that helps the business grow.

---

[13] Reichheld, Frederick F. and W. Earl Sasser, Jr., "Zero Defections: Quality Comes to Services," *Harvard Business Review*, September-October 1990, pp. 105-111.

NICKEL AND DIME DECISIONS

Realizing the value of satisfied customers is crucial when you are developing guidelines to deal with customers. For example, how many customer-contact employees will you need so that customers will not face prolonged waits? Will products and services be priced to maximize the profitability of each sale? Will they be priced to encourage repeat sales? Will advertising and personal selling messages be realistic so as not to inflate customers' expectations? (Unmet expectations lead to dissatisfaction.) How strong of a guarantee will you offer to customers, (e.g., will dissatisfied customers be allowed to exchange purchases for a complete refund and with as little inconvenience as possible? Will it be easy or difficult for customers to do business with you)?

In thinking about the value of satisfied customers and keeping them for the long term, I am reminded of a story that illustrates the importance of not being too greedy in the short term, instead taking a long-term perspective of profitability. A five-year-old boy would visit his grandfather periodically. During each visit Gramps would pull his grandson aside and offer him a gift—a choice of either a "beautiful, shiny, fat nickel," or an "ugly, dull, little dime." Each time the child would choose the nickel, and each time Gramps would have a good laugh. This went on for some time but the little boy never would choose the dime. Finally, the five-year-old's older and presumably wiser brother confronted his younger sibling:

"You dummy. Don't you know that a dime is worth more than a nickel? You can buy twice as much candy with the dime, and even if you don't like the looks of the dime you can always exchange it for *two* nickels at the store. It's obvious the dime is worth more, so why do you keep choosing the nickel?"

The younger boy's response? He looked his brother in the eye and emphatically explained, "I know a dime is worth more than the nickel, but as soon as I pick the dime, Gramps will stop playing the game!" The youngster realized that although a dime was worth more than a nickel, a stream of nickels over time was worth far more than one dime. The decision to opt for the nickel was the best choice, but not the most obvious one.

Unfortunately, the *nickel vs. dime* scenario is played out all too often in business. This is one reason why so many businesses realize only lackluster profits, or none at all. For example, I recently observed a group of bowlers as they approached the front counter at a bowling center. They were paying for about twenty bowling games, more than twice the average number of games for a party their size. The attendant totaled the bill on the cash register—$32.00. When one of the ladies in the group reached into her purse to retrieve the payment, she found a coupon for a free game of bowling at the center. After laying the coupon on the counter, she became disgruntled when the employee explained that he could not accept the coupon because he had already rung the amount on the cash register. "Coupons must be presented *before* the amount is tallied," he quipped. In protest, the lady paid the full amount and stormed out of the bowling center—perhaps never to return. The employee had chosen the *dime* rather than the *nickel*.

MARKETING ACTIVITIES

While the objective of marketing is profitably satisfying customers, a number of specific marketing activities facilitate the exchange process. The same research techniques discussed in Chapter 2 may be used to investigate the appropriateness of the multitude of decision alternatives associated with each of these activities. Broadly categorized, these marketing activities involve:

1. Selection of *target markets*

2. Determination of *product* offerings

3. *Pricing* the products and services

4. Developing a *promotional* plan

5. Evaluating and coordinating *distribution* alternatives

Selection of Target Markets

It is usually a mistake to try to be all things to all people. Select one or a few potential customer groups (i.e., *target markets*) and focus your marketing efforts on these groups. A separate marketing program may be necessary for each group. Select your target markets on the basis of your ability to serve them, relative to the competition's ability to serve them. Of course, target markets also should be substantial enough to be profitable and you must be able to identify and reach them.

There is almost no end to the number of ways a market might be segmented in search of the ideal target market(s). You might choose to examine *age* or *income* groups. For example, are seniors well served by competitors? Is there a potential to develop a children's version of the product? Are higher-income consumers well served? And so on.

Geography is another possibility, especially for retail stores and service businesses that require the presence of the customer. That is, are consumers in some neighborhoods currently inconvenienced by having to travel several miles to a competitor's place of business? If so, the prospective customers might be *intercepted* by opening your business between their neighborhoods and the competitor's business.

Some businesses select target markets on the basis of *customer benefits sought*. For example, if you are planning to open a health club, is it more desirable to appeal to a casual segment of the community who may be very interested in the social benefits of the club, or to a high-involvement group of consumers who may be more interested in the health benefits? The answer, of course, depends upon the number of consumers in each group and the number of competitors scrambling to serve them. The target market you select will influence your other marketing decisions, your operations and your competitors' reactions.

A frequent mistake is pursuing a target market that is too competitive, even though the enormous size of the market segment makes it appear to be very profitable. For example, it is generally more advantageous to appeal to a $1 million market segment not currently served by the competition, than to tackle a

$12 million segment already adequately served by a dozen well-entrenched competitors who may have a significant competitive edge (by virtue of having been in business for years). Pepsi Cola finally realized this principle about twenty years ago when they curtailed efforts to compete directly against Coca Cola in the adult market; instead, they emphasized appeals targeted toward younger consumers, dubbed *the Pepsi generation*.

Product Decisions

A *product* is more than a tangible object. In fact, for many service businesses there is little or nothing tangible about the product. Rather, a product is a *bundle of benefits* offered to the customer. The bundle might include the object's physical properties such as style, distinctive features, options, colors and quality, but also such benefits as delivery, installation, warranty, usage instructions and so on. Decisions concerning the composition of the benefit bundle are marketing-relevant because they are directly tied to the customer's satisfaction with the business. Shoddy or inappropriate products turn off would-be customers and, in the long run, cannot be offset by reduced prices, increased advertising or other substitute efforts.

Pricing

Pricing decisions can be difficult; yet they are unavoidable. Every product or service must have a price, even if the price is *free*. The search for the ideal price is complicated by the fact that each group of customers served may have a different idea about what constitutes a fair price. This is another reason it is useful to avoid appealing simultaneously to too many target markets. And if the competition slashes their prices, or if there is a downturn in the economy, your prices, which might have been viewed as reasonable last week, may not be so well received next week.

Despite the impossibility of determining the perfect price, the challenge of formulating a pricing strategy is made easier by considering several factors:

Costs

In the long term, your prices must at least cover your costs of doing business. These include *variable costs*, such as labor and materials used to manufacture each product, as well as *fixed costs,* such as rent, insurance and secretarial assistance that remain the same regardless of the volume of your business. Make sure you know these costs so you will not set your prices too low.

Objectives

What role do you want pricing to play in your overall marketing and business strategy? For example, lower prices might be necessary to gain a strong foothold in the marketplace and to deter would-be competitors. Conversely, higher prices might be appropriate if you are trying to foster an air of product exclusivity and prestige. As a third example, a discount granted to frequent or high-volume customers may help to solidify their loyalty.

Competition

What does the competition offer and how much do they charge? You may be able to charge a premium price if your business offers consumer benefits that competitors do not. Superior quality, faster delivery, better warranties, wider varieties and more flexible financing are a few examples. On the other hand, if there are few new customers to be found, you may elect to charge a low price to lure customers from the competition. If you beat the competitor's price, however, expect retaliatory reaction.

Systems price

What is the total price the customer must pay to purchase your product, including postage/freight, personal transportation, parking, long distance phone charges, etc.? Might there be ways to minimize these expenses to make your product more competitive? For example, a hair stylist might invest in a few toys and partition a corner of the shop for small children; then busy Moms can bring their children to the beauty parlor and avoid the cost of babysitters.

Market Demand

How price sensitive are potential customers? If a lower price increases the quantity that customers buy, it may be more profitable to keep prices low. Avoid drastic price discounts though, because consumers often equate price with quality. For example, who would want to purchase a set of dentures advertised for $19.95? Also avoid prices that are higher than the market's perception of a fair price. The price customers may be willing to pay one time may not be the same price they are willing to pay on a regular basis.

Communication

How well will the other elements of the marketing arsenal be used to communicate pricing decisions to customers? One technique is to break the price into smaller, more palatable increments. For example, a customer may object to a $5,000 price tag for a new photo copier, but may realize it is a good value at less than one cent per copy over the equipment's life. Another approach is to promote the price as being discounted from other reference prices such as those charged by competitors or—for retail stores—those prices recommended by manufacturers.

Non-monetary Prices

How much time, inconvenience or anxiety must customers pay to acquire and use your products? Could these be lowered to increase the perceived value of the product or service? Convenience stores, for example, tend to command higher prices than larger grocery stores because customer waiting time is cut to a minimum.

Pricing decisions extend beyond determining that the product should sell for $30, $40 or some other amount. For example, you might consider discounts for early payments, promotional assistance or quantity purchases. When should the price be lowered or raised? Should products be priced by the unit, by the dozen, or by some other standard? For example, a busy restaurant in New York charges customers by the meal and by the hour! Will additional charges be made for services such as delivery and installation, or will these services be included in the base price? How many days will each credit customer have to pay—*if* some customers are granted credit? Will the business accept checks, major credit cards or bartering? Should the customer pay before or after receiving the product or service? Consider each of these issues before opening your business.

Promotion

Contrary to popular belief, if you build a better mousetrap, the world will *not* necessarily beat a path to your door. Regardless of the superiority of your products, consumers will not be motivated to purchase until they are informed of your mousetrap's availability and virtues. The entrepreneur must use promotional tools to keep consumers informed.

Dozens of promotional alternatives exist, each with distinctive advantages and disadvantages. Broadly categorized, these promotional tools include:

Advertising

These are paid and nonpersonal communication, usually directed toward a mass audience by an identified business. Radio, television, magazines, direct mail and billboards are common advertising media. Advertising is especially appropriate when trying to generate marketplace awareness of your business.

When investing in advertising, avoid the temptation to cram too much information into each ad. Instead, emphasize the name of the business and one or two key points. Otherwise prospective customers will *tune out* the message. Also, make sure each ad runs several times, to increase the likelihood of impact; rarely will a single placement ad be sufficient to catch consumers' attention, create consumer awareness, instill an understanding and belief in the message, stimulate the consumer's intent to purchase, and then motivate the consumer to act on the intention. Finally, when selecting advertising media, avoid those with a great deal of *waste*, i.e., those that reach a high proportion of consumers outside of your target markets. Reputable media should be able to precisely describe their audience, so feel free to ask.

Personal Selling

These are oral presentations to prospective customers with the intent of making a sale. Although time consuming, personal selling can make a much stronger impression on potential customers than any other form of promotion. It is especially useful for closing the sale after advertising has heightened the customer's awareness and sparked his or her interest. It is also a key promotional tool when the product or service is nonstandardized and must be specially designed for each customer, when there are only a few customers in the target market, and when each prospective customer and each sale is extremely valuable.

In preparation for making sales calls, develop a sales call planner such as the one illustrated on the next page. This form will help you organize your sales calls and to remember the results of each call. It is also a good idea to make a list of questions and objections sales prospects might raise and how you would like to respond to each one.

One of the biggest reasons new salespeople fail to get the sale is because they do not ask for it; jot down a few different ways you might ask for the sale, e.g., "Would you prefer the blue unit or the red one?" "Will that be cash or charge?" "When would you like that delivered?" If employees will also be making sales calls, it is a good idea to organize this information into a sales manual to help train the salespeople.

Your Turn

A useful personal selling exercise is to role play a sales presentation with a friend who is knowledgeable enough to play the role of a prospective customer. Before beginning, instruct your partner to avoid making a purchase commitment. Instead, have him or her raise numerous questions and purchase objections. This will help you to learn how to best respond to whatever obstacles real sales prospects might raise.

CUSTOMER SALES CALL PLANNER[14]

1. Name: _____

   Address: _____

2. Type of business: _____

   Name of buyer: _____

3. People who influence buying decision or aid in selling our product: _____

4. Buying hours and best time to see buyer: _____

5. Receptionist's name: _____

6. Buyer's profile: _____

7. Sales call objectives: _____

8. What are customer's important buying needs? _____

9. Sales presentation

   A. Sales approach: _____

   B. Features, advantages, benefits: _____

   C. Method of demonstrating: features, advantages & benefits:

   _____

   D. How to relate benefits to customer's needs: _____

   E. Trial close to use: _____

   F. Anticipated objections: _____

   G. Trial close to use: _____

   H. How to close this customer: _____

   I. Hard or soft close: _____

10. Sales made—product use/promotional plan agreed upon: _____

    _____

11. Post sales call comments (reason did/did not buy; what to do on next call; follow-up promised): _____

[14] Source: Futrell, Charles M., *Fundamentals of Selling*, 3rd ed., Homewood, IL: Richard D. Irwin, Inc., 1990, p. 189

Sales Promotions

These are short-term inducements to stimulate traffic and/or sales. Coupons, free samples, sweepstakes, point-of-purchase displays, rub-off cards and free gifts are examples of commonly used sales promotions. These are great devices to encourage prospective customers to give your product a chance, or to get consumers in the door to take a closer look at what you have to offer. Unlike other forms of promotion, once sales promotions end, their impact generally ends. To ensure a lasting effect, sales promotions are best used in conjunction with other forms of promotion.

Publicity

This stimulates awareness and interest through mass media and through individuals who are usually not directly paid by the business. News items, announcements and stories about the business, its new products, and its employees, generate publicity—as do word-of-mouth communications that spread from customer to customer. Because the business does not directly pay for publicity, it is often very economical. Consumers tend to perceive it as a credible source of information. On the downside, publicity cannot be controlled as directly as other forms of promotion, so it may sometimes be unfavorable. Solid relations with the community, media and customers generally enhance the odds of generating favorable publicity.

As you plan the business' opening, consider capitalizing upon the opportunity to generate publicity by staging a grand opening celebration. Obviously, promote the event to prospective customers, but also to the media. Remember, however, that the goal of the media is not to generate publicity, per se, but to report newsworthy events of interest to their respective audiences. So, communicate the uniqueness of your business, products and services, how the business will help boost the local economy by employing several people, and in general how your new business will help to benefit the community. If possible, invite local celebrities to the grand opening; if they attend, media representatives are likely to follow.

Distribution

Distribution decisions involve activities that move the product and the product's title from the producer to the ultimate consumer. These include:

Location

Location of the business is especially important for most retail and service firms. (Review the discussion of location and site selection in Chapter 4.)

Channel Selection

It has often been said that a business can be only as good as its channel partners (i.e., suppliers and intermediary customers). For example, the quality and the reputation of an appliance manufacturer will suffer if the firm's supplier of electric motors delivers substandard motors. Conversely, a manufacturer who coordinates a network of reputable, dependable suppliers, wholesalers and retailers can often gain market access more quickly, more efficiently, more extensively and with less expense, less risk and greater customer satisfaction than might otherwise be possible. The first chart that follows illustrates a few examples of common channels of distribution. *Manufacturers and Middlemen: A Perfect Working Relationship,* follows and highlights the importance of establishing strong working relationships with channel members.

Intensity

Distribution might be intensive if your objective is to make the product widely available to gain market share, or if consumers are typically not brand loyal to products in the product category. On the other hand, a more selective or exclusive distribution strategy might be appropriate if the product will be truly unique, will have a prestige image, is highly sought by customers, or if manufacturing capacity is limited.

Physical Transport

How will the product be shipped to middlemen and to end customers (e.g., freight, rail, air)? How quickly will the product

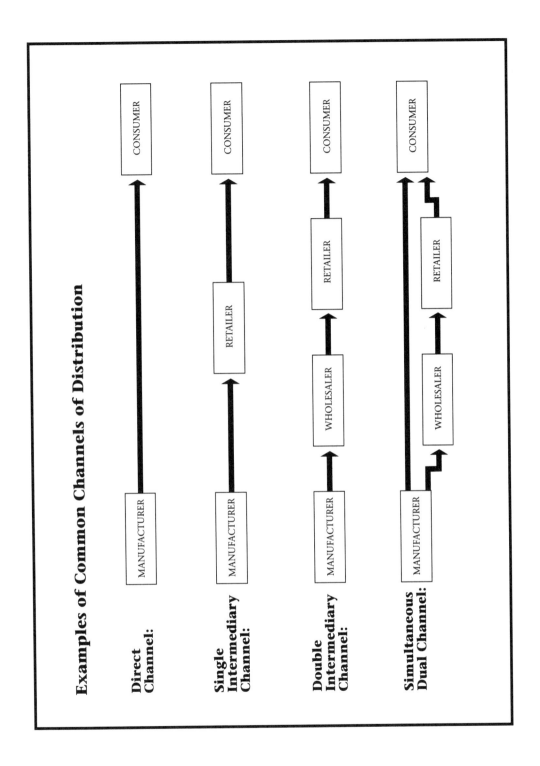

Examples of Common Channels of Distribution

Direct Channel:

MANUFACTURER → CONSUMER

Single Intermediary Channel:

MANUFACTURER → RETAILER → CONSUMER

Double Intermediary Channel:

MANUFACTURER → WHOLESALER → RETAILER → CONSUMER

Simultaneous Dual Channel:

MANUFACTURER → WHOLESALER → RETAILER → CONSUMER

be shipped (e.g., overnight express, next week)? What will be the minimum quantity shipped? How will the products be packaged for shipment? Again, you are wise to resolve these issues *before* opening your business, although they may be fine-tuned continuously thereafter.

MANUFACTURERS AND MIDDLEMEN: A PERFECT WORKING RELATIONSHIP[15]

The perfect middleman:

1. Has access to the market that the manufacturer wants to reach.

2. Carries an adequate inventory of the manufacturer's products and a satisfactory assortment of other products.

3. Has an effective promotional program—advertising, personal selling, and product displays. Promotional demands placed on the manufacturer are in line with what the manufacturer intends to do.

4. Provides services to customers—credit, delivery, installation and product repair—and honors the product warranty conditions.

The perfect manufacturer:

1. Provides a desirable assortment of products—well designed, properly priced, attractively packaged and delivered on time and in adequate quantities.

2. Builds product demand for these products by advertising their unique features and benefits.

3. Furnishes promotional assistance to its middlemen.

4. Provides managerial assistance for its middlemen.

5. Honors product warranties and provides repair and installation service.

The perfect combination:

1. Probably does not exist.

---

[15] Source: *Fundamentals of Marketing*, 8th ed., William J. Stanton and Charles Futrell, New York: McGraw Hill, 1987, p. 380. Reproduced with permission of McGraw Hill, Inc.

ASK YOURSELF

► What is "marketing"? What do marketers do?

► Why is it almost impossible for a business to survive with only one-time customers?

► What are three attractive target markets your business might appeal to? How might you reach them?

► How might you effectively promote your business on a limited budget?

PURCHASING
AND
INVENTORY
CONTROL

CHAPTER TEN

WHERE
IS IT?

"The peculiar thing about many businesses, both large and small, is the extreme care with which cash is guarded and the lack of care exercised over 'cash' in the form of inventories."

Clifford M. Baumback & Kenneth Lawyer

Manufacturers must maintain an inventory of raw materials and component parts to keep the production lines moving. They need to have finished goods available to fill orders. Retail stores must have ample merchandise on hand to resell to end users. And all businesses must keep an adequate supply of maintenance and office supplies to keep operations running smoothly. Therefore, dealing with purchasing and inventory tasks cannot be avoided.

Total inventory costs can be staggering. Sometimes this represents the largest cash outlay required to start the business. And as the business grows, the amount of cash tied up in inventory tends to increase. Despite the sizable cash investment, inventory usually cannot be as easily safeguarded in a tightly controlled bank vault like cash. Effective and efficient purchasing and inventory systems are mandatory. And such systems can prove to be very profitable—savings from these functions go directly to the bottom line. That is, a $1,000 decrease in purchasing and inventory costs increases net profit by $1,000, whereas a five-fold—or greater—increase in sales might be necessary to generate a similar increase in net profit. Moreover, a well managed purchasing and inventory system can minimize the headaches and lost revenues associated with substandard resale items, raw materials and supplies, as well as problems of late deliveries, stock-outs and obsolete merchandise.

Fortunately, help is available for setting up purchasing and inventory control systems. Suppliers, for example, realize that helping their customers is in their best interests. Many suppliers simplify purchasing tasks by accepting orders over their toll free "800" lines, by providing periodic statements and status reports of purchases, and by alerting customers when shortages may occur. Many suppliers will physically check inventory levels for customers and automatically reorder depleted items. Some have developed inventory control systems that they are willing to share with customers. Miller Brewing Company, for example, has written a convenient paper and pencil inventory control system that its tavern and restaurant customers can use to monitor stocks of alcoholic beverages.

Still, the ultimate responsibility for purchasing and inventory control rests with the entrepreneur. Therefore, Barker, Hovey and Murphy[16] offer seven key questions to consider when establishing a purchasing system:

1. Have you established specific policies and procedures regarding who will be authorized to purchase goods or services? Receive sales representative calls? Place requisitions? Process records?

2. Have you discussed your purchasing function with other firms or with local trade associations to obtain suggestions and/or techniques?

3. Have you requested prices from several vendors for each item or service you will purchase?

4. Have you visited or investigated potential vendors to verify that they can meet your requirements in terms of price, quality, quantity and service?

5. Does the volume of purchasing for any particular item warrant your dealing directly with its manufacturer— rather than with middlemen?

6. Do vendors have regular and competent sales personnel?

7. Do you anticipate problems with suppliers in regard to shortages? Backdoor selling? Delivery delays? Unsolicited favors or gifts?

---

[16] Source: *Management Audit for Small Service Firms,* Phillis A. Barker, David H. Hovey and John J. Murphy, Washington, D.C.: U.S. Small Business Administration, 1976, pp. 37-39.

MANAGING INVENTORY COSTS

Determining the right amount of inventory is difficult. If inventory levels are inadequate, shortages may occur that could translate into lost business, higher costs and anxiety associated with frequent reordering and dissatisfied customers whose loyalty may be difficult to recoup. The costs of excessive inventory also may be high, and often *hidden*. For example:

1. Financing costs—the interest expense associated with purchases. An extra $10,000 of inventory at a 12 percent rate of interest costs the business $100 every month.

2. Opportunity costs—alternative, income-producing use of money tied-up in inventory. For example, less inventory might free-up enough cash to upgrade the business' computing or telecommunications system.

3. Storage costs—when the space to store inventory must be leased or purchased. There may also be additional opportunity costs here; space used to store inventory might be used more productively for another purpose.

4. Insurance costs—which increase as more inventory is carried.

5. Obsolescence costs—the lost sales that occur when *new and improved* models are introduced and consumers no longer want the *old* items in your inventory. These costs can be substantial for retail businesses such as clothing stores.

6. Shrinkage costs—those losses due to breakage, damage, spoilage or theft. The longer an item sits in inventory, the greater the likelihood of shrinkage. Shoplifting and employee theft cost U.S. businesses more than $10 billion annually.

To help balance the trade-off between insufficient and excessive inventories, the economic order quantity (EOQ) has been developed. This powerful tool calculates the most economical number of units to be purchased per order. Generally, the ideal inventory level for each item should not exceed the EOQ—plus a modest safety stock to offset upward fluctuations in demand.

The EOQ uses this formula:

$$EOQ = \sqrt{\frac{2SV}{IC}}$$

where:

S = Estimated annual sales (in units)

V = Variable costs to place an order

I = Inventory holding costs, as a proportion of average inventory

C = Cost of one item

If S = 1,000, V = $20, I = .20 and C = $30, then:

$$EOQ = \sqrt{\frac{(2)\ (1000)\ (20)}{(.2)\ (30)}} = 81.66$$

Under this scenario, the ideal order would be about 82 units each time the inventory is replenished. Ordering more or fewer than 82 units becomes uneconomical.

In other ordering situations, additional factors complicate the EOQ calculation. For example, if the supplier offers quantity discounts for high-volume purchases, several EOQs might be calculated with the inventory holding (I) and item costs (C) adjusted in each computation to reflect the altered costs at each purchase volume level.

ASK YOURSELF

► Referring to the quote at the beginning of the chapter, why are some businesses careless with inventories?

► Why might the required investment in inventory, raw materials and supplies grow as the business grows?

► What are the negative consequences of having too *much* inventory on hand at any given moment? What are the negative consequences of having too *little* inventory on hand?

CHAPTER ELEVEN

RECORD KEEPING

WHAT IS THE SCORE?

Although you could postpone some record keeping decisions until after the start-up, in the long-run you will save yourself time and headaches if you determine, in advance, what paperwork and accounting records you need. Paperwork considerations are important in a strategic and tactical context. They affect:

► The way employees perform their jobs

► The accountability of employees

► Customer service

► The owner's ability to monitor business operations

► The accuracy of tax filings and compliance with other governmental information requirements

► The quality of the owner's business decisions

► The ability to raise additional capital

► Long-term planning

► Profitability and business success

Specific record keeping needs vary from business to business, but every system should provide needed and meaningful information. It should be easy to use and understand, reliable, inexpensive, accurate, consistent and timely—yet, not unnecessarily time-consuming. A typical record keeping system would include records for:

1. Sales

2. Cash receipts

3. Cash disbursements

4. Accounts receivable

5. Accounts payable

6. Physical assets (including depreciation)

7. Insurance

8. Personnel (including payroll)

9. Customers and potential customers

10. Suppliers and other creditors

11. Production and inventory

12. Miscellaneous correspondence

What an Owner-Manager Should Know, that follows, is a financial status check list to help assess whether or not your financial bookkeeping system provides adequate information. Numerous commercial systems—hard copy and software—are available to help you keep these and other financial records. Your accountant and/or local office supply store should be able to suggest which of these systems are best suited for your business.

SMALL BUSINESS FINANCIAL STATUS CHECKLIST[17]

(What an Owner-Manager Should Know)

DAILY

1. Cash on hand.

2. Bank Balance—keep business and personal funds separate.

3. Daily Summary of sales and cash receipts.

4. That all errors in recording collections on accounts are corrected.

5. That a record of all monies paid out, by cash or check, is maintained.

WEEKLY

1. Accounts Receivable—take action on slow payers.

2. Accounts Payable—take advantage of discounts.

3. Payroll—records should include name and address of employee, social security number, number of exemptions, date ending the pay period, hours worked, rate of pay, total wages, deductions, net pay, check number.

4. Taxes and reports to State and Federal Government—sales, withholding, social security, etc.

---

[17]Source: *Keeping Records in Small Business,* John Cotton, U.S. Small Business Administration, Management Aid #1.017, 1985.

MONTHLY

1. That all Journal entries are classified according to like elements—these should be generally accepted and standardized for both income and expense—and posted to General Ledger.

2. That a Profit and Loss Statement for the month is available within a reasonable time, usually ten to fifteen days following the close of the month. This shows the income for the business for the month, the expense incurred in obtaining the income, and the profit or loss resulting. From this, take action to eliminate loss—adjust mark-up? reduce overhead expense? pilferage? incorrect tax reporting? incorrect buying procedures? failure to take advantage of cash discounts?

3. That a Balance Sheet accompanies the Profit and Loss Statement. This shows assets (what the business has), liabilities (what the business owes) and the investment of the owner.

4. The Bank Statement is reconciled. That is, the owner's books are in agreement with the bank's record of the cash balance.

5. The Petty Cash Account is in balance. The actual cash in the Petty Cash Box, plus the total of the paid-out slips that have not been charged to expense, total the amount set aside as petty cash.

6. That all Federal Tax Deposits, withheld income and FICA taxes (Form 501) and State Taxes are made.

7. That Accounts Receivable are aged (i.e., thirty, sixty, ninety days, etc., past due). Work all bad and slow accounts.

8. That Inventory Control is worked to remove dead stock and order new stock. What moves slowly? Reduce. What moves fast? Increase.

Keep in mind that many non-financial records also may be of great value—for example, records of employee performance evaluations, customer lists including addresses and phone numbers, customer inquiries and complaints, insurance policies, information provided by suppliers, and so on. If you open your business without a plan to systematically collect and organize needed records, you could quickly become paralyzed in a nightmare of paperwork.

Developing a personal time management system may be another useful set of records to keep. First, you will have a firmer grasp as to how much time each task in the business takes, so you will have a basis to determine how many employees you will need and what level of productivity each should achieve. Second, your sensitivity to finding faster, more time efficient ways of accomplishing tasks also may be heightened. Finally, by documenting how you spend your time, you will be able to make more informed decisions as you gradually reprioritize and reallocate the way your time is spent. Such decisions may involve an increased amount of delegation to employees. Or, you might make a personal commitment to devote a certain amount of time each day interacting with customers, or reserve a block of time, on a regular basis, to deal with long-term issues and opportunities facing the business.

ASK YOURSELF

► Why is record keeping an essential activity for entrepreneurs?

► What records should be kept?

CHAPTER TWELVE

SPREADING
THE RISK
WITH
INSURANCE

REDUCING THE RISK

"Where profit is, loss is hidden nearby."
Japanese Proverb

This final discussion of strategic and tactical considerations involved in the small business planning process deals with risk. Risk is an accepted reality in American business. It is omnipresent. Some entrepreneurs thrive upon risk; they find it provides excitement and challenge. Others find risk to be anxiety-producing; for them, the uncertainties and potential for loss associated with risk are intolerable.

Fortunately for risk averse entrepreneurs, some risk can be reduced. For example, learning about the customer's needs reduces the risk of offering a product no one will purchase. Adopting safety measures reduces the risk of fire and injury in your business. When the risk cannot be reduced totally, it can often be transferred to someone else—through insurance. Before opening your business, consult with one or more insurance agents. Otherwise, you may be risking more than you can afford to lose.

According to the Small Business Administration, four types of insurance are essential, while nine other types may be desirable—depending on the business and the entrepreneur's aversion to risk.

▶ Essential insurance coverages

- Fire
- Liability
- Automobile
- Worker's Compensation

▶ Desirable insurance coverages

- Business interruption
- Crime
- Glass
- Rent
- Group life

- Group health
- Disability
- Retirement income
- Key-man

The *Insurance Coverage Checklist* that follows outlines a few key considerations associated with each kind of insurance coverage. Review it before you meet with insurance agents.

Insurance Coverage Checklist[18]

FIRE INSURANCE	No action needed	Look into this
1. Other perils—such as windstorm, hail, smoke, explosion, vandalism and malicious mischief—can be added to your basic fire insurance at a relatively small additional cost.	_____	_____
2. If you need comprehensive coverage, your best buy may be one of the all-risk contracts that offer the broadest available protection for the money.	_____	_____
3. The insurance company may indemnify you—that is, compensate you for your losses—in any one of several ways: (1) It may pay actual cash value of the property at the time of loss; (2) it may repair or replace the property with material of kind and quality or (3) it may take all the property at the agreed or appraised value and reimburse you for your loss.	_____	_____
4. You can insure property you do not own. You must have an insurable interest—that is, a financial interest—in the property when a loss occurs, but not necessarily at		

---

[18]Source: *Insurance Checklist for Small Business*, Mark R. Green, Small Business Administration.

the time the insurance contact is made. For instance, a repair shop or a dry-cleaning plant may carry insurance on customers' property in the shop, or a person holding a mortgage on a building may insure the building, although he or she does not own it. ____ ____

5. When you sell property, you cannot assign the insurance policy along with the property, unless you have permission from the insurance company. ____ ____

6. Even if you have several policies on your property, you can still collect only the amount of your actual cash loss. All the insurers share the payment proportionately. For example, suppose that you are carrying two policies—one for $20,000 and one for $30,000—on a $40,000 building, and a fire causes damage to the building, amounting to $12,000.

The $20,000 policy will pay $4,800; that is:

$$\frac{20{,}000}{50{,}000} \text{ or } \frac{2}{5} \text{' of } \$12{,}000 = \$4{,}800$$

The $30,000 policy will pay $7,200; which is:

$$\frac{30{,}000}{50{,}000} \text{ or } \frac{3}{5} \text{' of } \$12{,}000 = \$7{,}200$$ ____ ____

7. Special protection other than the standard fire policy is needed to cover the loss by fire of accounts, bills, currency, deeds, evidences of debt, and money and securities. ____ ____

8. If an insured building is vacant or unoccupied for more than sixty consecutive days, coverage is suspended unless you have a special endorsement to your policy canceling this provision. ____ ____

9. If, either before or after a loss, you conceal or misrepresent to the insurer any material fact or circumstance concerning your insurance or the interest of the insured, the policy may be voided. _____ _____

10. If you increase the hazard of fire, the insurance company may suspend your coverage, even for losses not originating from the increased hazard. (An example of such a hazard might be renting part of your building to a dry-cleaning plant.) _____ _____

11. After a loss, you must use all reasonable means to protect the property from further loss, or run the risk of having your coverage canceled. _____ _____

12. To recover your loss, you must furnish—within sixty days—unless an extension is granted by the insurance company—a complete inventory of the damaged, destroyed and undamaged property, showing in detail the quantities, costs, actual cash value and amount of loss claimed. _____ _____

13. If you and the insurer disagree on the amount of loss, the question may be resolved through special appraisal procedures provided for in the insurance policy. _____ _____

14. You may cancel your policy without notice at any time and get part of the premium returned. The insurance company also may cancel at any time but it must give you a five-day written notice. _____ _____

15. By accepting a co-insurance clause in your policy, you can get a substantial reduction in premiums. A co-insurance clause states that you must carry insurance equal to 80

percent or 90 percent of the value of the insured property. If you carry less than this, you cannot collect the full amount of your loss, even if the loss is small. The percent of your loss that you can collect will depend on the percent of the full value of the property you have had insured. _____ _____

16. If your loss is caused by someone else's negligence, the insurer has the right to sue this negligent third party for the amount it has paid you under the policy. This is known as the insurer's right of subrogation. However, the insurer will usually waive this right upon request. For example, if you have leased your insured building to some-one and have waived your right to recover from the tenant for any insured damages to your property, you should have your agent request the insurer to waive the subrogation clause in the fire policy on your leased building. _____ _____

17. A building under construction can be insured for fire, lightning, extended cover-age, vandelism and malicious mischief. _____ _____

LIABILITY INSURANCE

1. Legal liability limits of $1 million are no longer considered high or unreasonable, even for a small business. _____ _____

2. Most liability policies require you to notify the insurer immediately after any incident on your property that might cause a future claim. This holds true no matter how unim-portant the incident may seem at the time it happens. _____ _____

3. Most liability policies, in addition to bodily injuries, may now cover personal injuries —libel, slander and so on—if these are specifically stated in the policy. _____ _____

4. Under certain conditions, your business may be subject to damage claims, even from trespassers.   _____   _____

5. You may be legally liable for damages, even in cases in which you used "reasonable care."   _____   _____

6. Even if the suit against you is false or fradulent, the liability insurer pays court costs, legal fees and interest on judgments, in addition to the liability judgments themselves.   _____   _____

7. You can be liable for the acts of others, under contracts you have signed with them. This liability is insurable.   _____   _____

8. In some cases you may be held liable for fire loss to property of others in your care. Yet, this property would normally not be covered by your fire or general liability insurance. This risk can be covered by fire legal liability insurance or through requesting subrogation waivers from insurers of owners of the property.   _____   _____

AUTOMOBILE INSURANCE

1. When an employee or a subcontractor uses his or her own car on your behalf, you can be legally liable even if you do not own a car or truck yourself.   _____   _____

2. Five or more automobiles or motorcycles under one ownership that are operated as a fleet for business purposes can generally be insured under a low-cost fleet policy against both material damage to the vehicles and liability to others for property damage or personal injury.   _____   _____

3. You can often get deductibles of almost any amount—say $250 or $500—and thereby reduce your premiums. _____ _____

4. Automobile medical-payments insurance pays for medical claims, including your own, arising from automobile accidents, regardless of the question of negligence. _____ _____

5. In most states, you must carry liability insurance or be prepared to provide other proof—such as surety bond—of financial responsibility when you are involved in an accident. _____ _____

6. You can purchase uninsured motorist protection to cover your own bodily-injury claims from someone who has no insurance. _____ _____

7. Personal property stored that is in an automobile and is not attached to it—for example, merchandise being delivered—is not covered under an automobile policy. _____ _____

WORKER'S COMPENSATION INSURANCE

1. Common law requires that an employer: (1) provide his or her employees a safe place to work, (2) hire competent fellow employees; (3) provide safe tools and (4) warn employees of any existing dangers. _____ _____

2. If an employer fails to provide the above, under both common law and worker's compensation laws, he or she is liable for damage suits brought by an employee. _____ _____

3. State law determines the level or type of benefits payable under worker's compensation policies. _____ _____

4. Not all employees are covered by worker's compensation laws. The exceptions are determined by state law, and therefore vary from state to state. _____ _____

5. In nearly all states, an employer is now legally required to cover his or her workers under worker's compensation. _____ _____

6. You can save money on worker's compensation insurance by seeing that your employees are properly classified. _____ _____

7. Rates for worker's compensation insurance vary from 0.1 percent of the payroll for "safe" occupations to about 25 percent or more of the payroll for very hazardous occupations. _____ _____

8. Most employers in most states can reduce their worker's compensation premium costs by reducing their accident rates below the average. They do this by using safety and loss prevention measures. _____ _____

BUSINESS INTERRUPTION INSURANCE

1. Insurance can be purchased to cover fixed expenses that would continue if a fire shut down your business—such as salaries to key employees, taxes, interest, depreciation and utilities—as well as the profits you would lose. _____ _____

2. Under properly written contingent business interruption insurance, you can also collect if fire or other peril closes down the business of a supplier or customer, which interrupts your business. _____ _____

3. The business interruption policy provides payments for amounts you spend to hasten the reopening of your business after a fire or other insured peril. _____ _____

4. You can get coverage for the extra expenses you suffer if an insured peril, while not actually closing your business down, seriously disrupts it. _____ _____

5. When the policy is properly endorsed, you can get business interruption insurance to indemnify you if your operations are suspended because of failure or interruption of the supply of power, light, heat, gas or water furnished by a public utility company.   _____ _____

CRIME INSURANCE

1. Burglary insurance excludes such property as accounts, articles in showcase windows and manuscripts.   _____ _____

2. Coverage is granted under burglary insurance only if there are visible marks of the burglar's forced entry.   _____ _____

3. Burglary insurance can be written to cover —in addition to money in a safe—inventoried merchandise and damage incurred in the course of a burglary.   _____ _____

4. Robbery insurance protects you from loss of property, money, and securities by force, trickery or threat of violence, on or off your premises.   _____ _____

5. A comprehensive crime policy, written just for small business owners, is available. In addition to burglary and robbery, it covers other types of loss by theft, destruction and disappearance of money and securities. It also covers thefts committed by your employees.   _____ _____

6. If you are in a high-risk area and cannot get insurance through normal channels without paying excessive rates, you may be able to get help through the federal crime insurance plan. Your agent or State Insurance Commissioner can tell you where to get information about these plans.   _____ _____

GLASS INSURANCE

1. You can purchase a special glass insurance policy that covers all risk to plate glass windows, glass signs, motion-picture screens, glass brick, glass doors, showcases, countertops and insulated glass panels. _____ _____

2. The glass insurance policy covers not only the glass itself, but also its lettering and ornamentation, if these are specifically insured, and the costs of temporary plates or boarding up when necessary. _____ _____

3. After the glass has been replaced, full coverage is continued without any additional premium for the period covered. _____ _____

RENT INSURANCE

1. You can buy rent insurance that will pay your rent if the property that you lease becomes unusable due to fire or other insured perils and if your lease calls for continued payments in such a situation. _____ _____

2. If you own property and lease it to others, you can insure against loss if the lease is canceled due to fire and you have to rent the property again at a reduced rental. _____ _____

DISABILITY INSURANCE

1. Worker's compensation insurance pays an employee only for time lost due to work-related injuries and illnesses—not for time lost due to disabilities incurred off the job. But you can purchase, at a low premium, insurance to replace the lost income of workers who suffer short-term or long-term disability that is not related to their work. _____ _____

2. You can get coverage that provides employees with an income for life in case of permanent disability resulting from work-related accident or illness. _____ _____

GROUP LIFE INSURANCE

1. If you pay group insurance premiums and cover all employees up to $50,000, the cost to you is deductible for federal income tax purposes; yet, the value of the benefit is not taxable income to your employees. _____ _____

2. Most insurers will provide group coverages at low rates, even if there are ten or fewer employees in your group. _____ _____

3. If employees pay part of the cost of the group insurance, state laws require that 75 percent of them must elect coverage for the plan to qualify as group insurance. _____ _____

4. Group plans permit an employee leaving the company to convert his or her group insurance coverage to a private plan, at the rate for his or her age, without a medical exam, if that person does so within thirty days after leaving the job. _____ _____

GROUP HEALTH INSURANCE

1. Group health insurance costs much less than would individual contracts, and it provides more generous benefits for the worker. _____ _____

2. If you pay the entire cost, individual employees cannot be dropped from a group plan unless the entire group policy is canceled. _____ _____

3. Generous programs of employee benefits, such as group health insurance, tend to reduce labor turnover. _____ _____

RETIREMENT INCOME

1. If you are self-employed, you can get an income tax deduction for funds used for retirement for you and your employees through plans of insurance or annuities approved for use under the Employees Retirement Income Security Act of 1974 (ERISA). _____ _____

| | *No action needed* | *Look into this* |

2. Annuity contracts may provide for variable payments in the hope of giving the annuitants some protection against the effects of inflation. Whether fixed or variable, an annuity can provide retirement income that is guaranteed for life. _____ _____

KEY MAN COVERAGE

1. One of the most serious setbacks that can come to a small company is the loss of a key person. But this person can be insured with life insurance and disability insurance owned by and payable to your company. _____ _____

2. Proceeds of a key-man coverage insurance policy, which accumulates as an asset of the business, can be borrowed against, and the interest and dividends are not subject to income tax as long as the policy remains in force. _____ _____

3. The cash value of key-man coverage insurance, which accumulates as an asset of the business, can be borrowed against—and the interest and dividends are not subject to income tax as long as the policy remains in force. _____ _____

ASK YOURSELF

▶ Which types of business insurance will you need for your new business?

▶ What are the consequences of *not* having insurance?

▶ What questions will you ask your insurance agent when you meet with him or her?

CHAPTER THIRTEEN

FORECASTS

AND

BUDGETS

THINKING AHEAD

After you formulate an extensive list of tentative strategic and tactical decisions for your small business, the next step in the planning process is to forecast revenues (presumably sales), costs and expenses, profits and cash. Preparing forecasts forces entrepreneurs to carefully consider the future financial position of their business. Doing so minimizes future surprises and crises. Though initial forecasts for new businesses are rarely as accurate as entrepreneurs would like, the more accurate the forecast, the more effectively you can plan, the more efficiently you can deploy resources, the better your customers can be served, and the more profitable your business will be.

SALES FORECASTING

Estimating future sales is probably the most critical forecast. All other forecasts and budgets are directly or indirectly derived from the sales forecast. If the sales forecast is significantly off, you will have problems in estimating the requirements for personnel, equipment, raw materials, profits and cash. Use a combination of the following techniques to forecast sales:

Industry norms, based upon census or trade association data for similar size and type of businesses. Industry trade associations and magazines often publish this type of information. Reference books such as *Robert Morris & Associates' Annual Statement Studies* and *Industry Norms & Key Business Ratios* also report industry norms. They can be found in many public libraries.

Partner/investor opinion. Ask key people who are helping you start your business; then, average their estimates.

User's expectations. If your business will serve only a few customers and you can identify them before the start-up, aggregate their estimates of what they expect to purchase. This method works best when the demand for your product is a *derived demand* (i.e., contingent upon the demand for your business customers' products). An example is the demand for milk cartons that is inseparably tied to the demand for milk. Be careful when interpreting these estimates, however, since some customers will inflate their forecasts to avoid a disruption in supply and/or to negotiate price concessions.

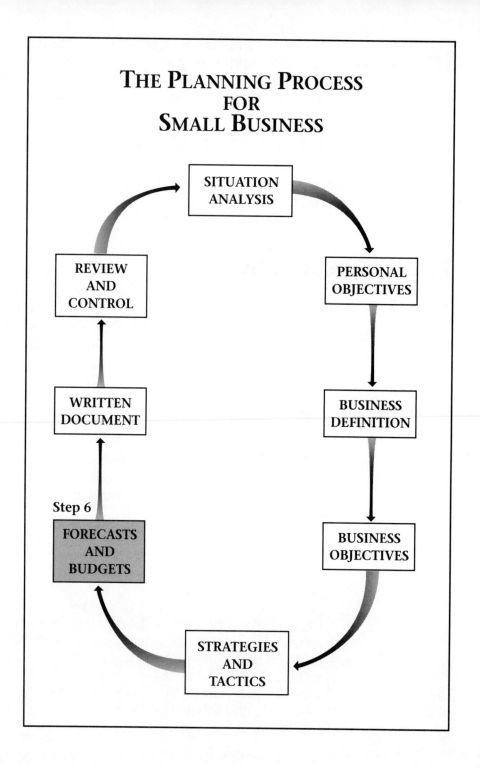

THE PLANNING PROCESS FOR SMALL BUSINESS

SITUATION ANALYSIS

PERSONAL OBJECTIVES

REVIEW AND CONTROL

BUSINESS DEFINITION

WRITTEN DOCUMENT

BUSINESS OBJECTIVES

Step 6

FORECASTS AND BUDGETS

STRATEGIES AND TACTICS

Competitor audits. For example, an entrepreneur opening a new restaurant might get some *feel* for demand by periodically counting the number of automobiles in the parking lots of competitors.

Simulated test markets. Some marketing research firms conduct artificial market tests in mock stores to assess the sales potential of new products and to help fine-tune marketing plans. Such services would be very expensive for most small business entrepreneurs—one such firm charges a minimum of $75,000 per market test. However, when launching new products on a national level, valuable insights may be gained from these market tests. The results could save a business considerable expense, which can often justify the cost of the market tests.

Direct mail sampling. For products to be sold through the mail, this economical technique tests portions of mailing lists before undertaking the expense of mass mailings.

PROFITABILITY FORECASTING

Profits may be estimated after the sales forecast has been made and after costs and expenses have been identified. A worksheet such as the *Estimated Projection and Forecast* sample that follows is handy for forecasting profits realized in a specific time period, such as a year. Of course, you should also itemize additional revenues and expenses particular to your individual business. The *Start-up Costs* worksheet, which follows, will help you identify start-up costs incurred before you open your business.

When computing profitability, it is sometimes enlightening to conduct a *sensitivity analysis*. In other words, consider a few "what if . . . ?" scenarios: What if sales—or costs or expenses—are 10 percent (20 percent, 30 percent, etc.) above or below your best estimate? A change in sales, costs or expenses will not always have a proportionately corresponding effect on profitability.

The *Worksheet for Balance Sheet* example that follows will be useful throughout the life of your business. The balance sheet provides an invaluable *snapshot* of the business' overall position at a *single point in time*. It effectively aggregates all of the profits, losses, assets and debts realized in previous periods.

ESTIMATED PROJECTION AND FORECAST OF THREE YEARS' EARNINGS[19]

	Year:	19__	19__	19__
Gross Receipts		____	____	____
Merchandise Cost		____	____	____
Gross Profit (Receipts less merch. cost)		____	____	____
Expenses				
Officers' Salaries (if corporation)		____	____	____
Employee Wages		____	____	____
Accounting & Legal Fees		____	____	____
Advertising		____	____	____
Rent		____	____	____
Depreciation		____	____	____
Supplies		____	____	____
Electricity		____	____	____
Telephone		____	____	____
Interest		____	____	____
Repairs		____	____	____
Taxes		____	____	____
Insurance		____	____	____
Bad Debts		____	____	____
**Miscellaneous (Postage, etc.)		____	____	____
Total Expenses		____	____	____
Net Profit (Gross Profit less total expenses)		____	____	____
Less Income Taxes (if corporation)		____	____	____
Net Profit After Taxes		____	____	____
Less Withdrawals (i.e., loan payments, Proprietorship/Partnership)		____	____	____
Net Profit		____	____	____

**If sum is large, please itemize.

---

[19] Source: Courtesy of the Small Business Administration

START-UP COSTS[20]

Money needed for owner or manager $ _____ Until opening

Living Expenses:

Moving Expenses	_____	Once
Salary for owner or manager	_____	1-3 months
Land (buy or lease)	_____	1-3 months
Building	_____	Once

Building Expenses:

Equipment	_____	Once
Fixtures	_____	Once
Decorating and remodeling	_____	Once
Salaries and wages	_____	1-3 months
Inventory	_____	1-3 months
Advertising	_____	3 months
Telephone	_____	1-3 months

Business Expenses:

Utilities	_____	1-3 months
Insurance	_____	As required
Legal and professional fees	_____	1-3 months
Vehicles	_____	Once
Supplies	_____	1-3 months
Starting inventory	_____	Once
Utility deposits	_____	Once
Licenses	_____	Once
Advertising & promotion for opening	_____	Once

Cash Reserve (Petty Cash; Credit Accounts) _____ 1-3 months

Total Cash Required to Start a Business $ _____

---

[20] Robert T. Justis, *Managing Your Small Business*, © 1981, p. 93, Reprinted by permission of Prentice-Hall, Inc., Englewood Cliffs, NJ.

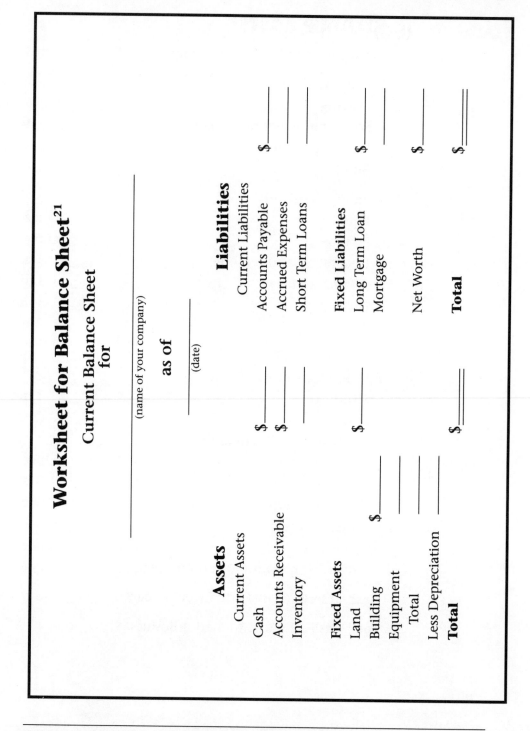

Worksheet for Balance Sheet[21]

Current Balance Sheet

for

_____
(name of your company)

as of

_____
(date)

Assets

Current Assets

Cash $ _____

Accounts Receivable $ _____

Inventory   _____

Fixed Assets

Land $ _____

Building   _____

Equipment   _____

Total   _____

Less Depreciation _____

Total $ _____

Liabilities

Current Liabilities

Accounts Payable $ _____

Accrued Expenses   _____

Short Term Loans   _____

Fixed Liabilities

Long Term Loan $ _____

Mortgage   _____

Net Worth $ _____

Total $ _____

---

[21] Source: Business Plan for Small Manufacturers, Management Aid #2.007, U.S. Small Business Administration, 1985.

CASH FORECASTING AND BUDGETING

Accurate cash flow projections are critical to the success of a new business. Just because a business is expected to be profitable does not necessarily mean that enough cash will be on hand to pay creditors, employees and taxes when the needs arise. Often, entrepreneurs invest their entire savings when they start a new business, and do not have a sufficient cushion of cash remaining to pay bills when they are due. Other entrepreneurs grow their businesses so rapidly that their businesses consume more cash than they generate. This is because increasingly larger amounts of cash become tied-up in inventory, equipment, facilities, payroll and accounts receivable. In either case, it is useful to think in terms of monitoring and managing cash as well as profits. A worksheet such as the *Estimated Cash Forecast* that follows is useful for estimating cash flows.

Estimated Cash Forecast[22]

	Jan	Feb	Mar	Apr	May	Jun	Jul	Aug
(1) Cash in Bank (Start of Month)								
(2) Petty Cash (Start of Month)								
(3) Total Cash (add (1) and (2))								
(4) Expected Accounts Receivable								
(5) Other Money Expected								
(6) Total Receipts (add (4) and (5))								
(7) Total Cash and Receipts (add (3) and (6))								
(8) All Disbursements (for month)								
(9) Cash Balance at End of Month in Bank Account and Petty Cash (subtract (8) from (7))*								

*This balance is your starting cash balance for the next month.

[22] Source: Ibid.

If you anticipate possible cash drains in advance, you can take several steps to avoid cash crises. For example, to increase cash in the *short* term, you may be able to plan ways to:

- ► Accelerate payments by your customers (e.g., offer discounts or other incentives to customers who pay early).

- ► Grant credit to fewer customers.

- ► Eliminate or postpone purchases from suppliers.

- ► Negotiate extended payment terms with creditors.

- ► Deplete inventories of raw materials and supplies before reordering.

- ► Reorder raw materials and supplies in smaller quantities.

- ► Arrange for a short-term line of credit from a local lending institution.

- ► Sell long overdue accounts receivable to a collection agency.

Chapter 15 addresses the need for long-term cash when you start your business and, eventually, to expand its operations.

ASK YOURSELF

► Why are forecasts and budgets useful?

► Why is the sales forecast prepared before other forecasts and budgets?

► Is your business plan flexible enough to allow for forecasting errors? In other words, what are the consequences of each forecast being off by X percent?

► Why are monthly profits not always the same as monthly cash flow? Why is it important to understand the distinction?

CHAPTER FOURTEEN

COMPLETING
THE
PLANNING
PROCESS

WRITE THE PLAN

Two steps remain in the small business planning process—writing the planning document, and reviewing and controlling the plan.

By this time, you have assembled hundreds of pieces of information and considered answers in response to the seemingly endless onslaught of questions raised in previous chapters. As well organized as your notes may be, and as clear as your thoughts are currently, at some point in the future—hopefully, at several points in the future—you will need to recall precisely what planning decisions you made and why. If partners, employees and potential investors are to play a significant role in the business, they too will need to understand your plans.

This next-to-last step in the small business planning process is to prepare a written document, to organize and clarify your business plans. In fact, it may be a good idea to write two plans—a detailed plan for yourself, and a shorter, condensed version for likely investors who may not be interested in the minute business details you have addressed.

The written plan should reflect the information gathered and the decisions made throughout the planning process—with two possible exceptions. First, you may not wish to include a section on your personal objectives. Second, if one purpose of the plan is to attract investors, some description of your background, experience and qualifications would be a plus—as well as corresponding profiles of the key employees you intend to hire. The *Sample Business Plan Outline* provides a sample outline of a written business plan.

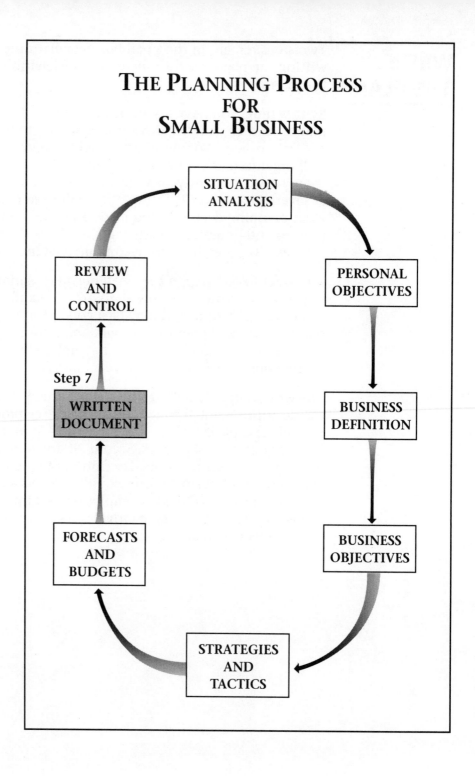

THE PLANNING PROCESS
FOR
SMALL BUSINESS

SITUATION ANALYSIS

PERSONAL OBJECTIVES

REVIEW AND CONTROL

Step 7
WRITTEN DOCUMENT

BUSINESS DEFINITION

BUSINESS OBJECTIVES

FORECASTS AND BUDGETS

STRATEGIES AND TACTICS

SAMPLE BUSINESS PLAN OUTLINE[23]

I. Summary

    A. Business description

        1. Name

        2. Location

        3. Product(s)

        4. Market and competition

        5. Management expertise

    B. Business definition, goals and objectives

    C. Summary of financial needs and application of funds

    D. Earnings projections and potential return to investors

II. Market Analysis

    A. Description of total market

    B. Industry trends

    C. Target market

    D. Competition

III. Products or Services

    A. Description of product line

    B. Proprietary position: patents, copyrights, legal and technical considerations

    C. Comparison to competitors' products, operations, facilities, quality

IV. Manufacturing Process (if applicable)

    A. Materials

    B. Source of supply

    C. Production methods

V. Marketing Strategy

    A. Overall strategy

    B. Pricing policy

    C. Method of selling, distributing and servicing products

---

[23] Source: Adapted from: "Financing Small Business," Bank of America *Small Business Reporter*, October, 1980, p. 19.

VI. Management Plan

    A. Form of business organization

    B. Board of directors composition

    C. Officers: organization chart and responsibilities

    D. Resumes of key personnel

    E. Staffing plan/number of employees

    F. Facilities plan/planned capital improvements

    G. Operating plan/schedule of upcoming work for next one to two years

VII. Financial Data

    A. Financial statements (five years to present)

    B. Five-year financial projections (first year by quarters; remaining years annually)

      1. Profit and loss statements

      2. Balance Sheets

      3. Cash flow charts

      4. Capital expenditure estimates

    C. Explanation of projections

    D. Key business ratios

VIII. Other Pertinent Information, Plans

REVIEW AND CONTROL

A common occurrence is for the entrepreneur to write a planning document, distribute copies to potential investors, obtain the required funding, and then set the plan on a shelf to collect dust. While there certainly is value to thinking through the planning process and then committing your thoughts to paper, the plan should also be utilized as an ongoing reference document. The final step is to refer to the written plan several times throughout the start-up process; then thoroughly review and revise the plan at least annually after you open the business.

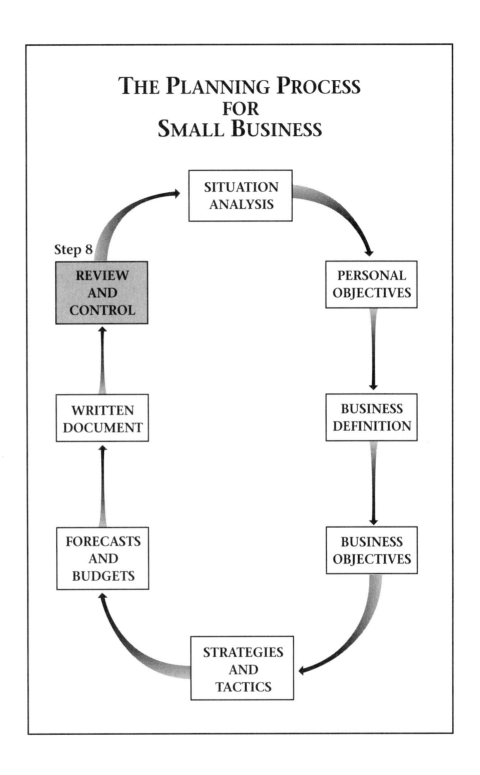

THE PLANNING PROCESS
FOR
SMALL BUSINESS

SITUATION
ANALYSIS

Step 8

REVIEW
AND
CONTROL

PERSONAL
OBJECTIVES

WRITTEN
DOCUMENT

BUSINESS
DEFINITION

FORECASTS
AND
BUDGETS

BUSINESS
OBJECTIVES

STRATEGIES
AND
TACTICS

During the start-up process, use the written document to focus upon at least three sets of issues. First, identify the sequence of tasks that need to be done before the business can open. What should be done first, second, third, etc.? Remember that some tasks may have to be initiated several weeks in advance of others to avoid needless downtime. For example, production equipment must be ordered, delivered and installed before employees can be trained to operate the equipment. Next, develop timetables for completing those tasks—holding yourself accountable for meeting specific deadlines. Finally, assign yourself—or partners, employees, consultants, accountants, contractors, etc.—the responsibility of completing the tasks—though ultimately *all* responsibility is yours.

After the start-up, invest some time reviewing and revising the plan. Have predetermined strategies and tactics been success-fully implemented? Have you met your stated objectives? If not, why not? Here are a few tips to consider as you review the plan:

► Do not be afraid to change your projections or assumptions if they appear unrealistic or if conditions change.

► Modify your strategies or operating decisions if they are not as effective as you originally envisioned.

However:

► Try to maintain some degree of continuity. Avoid drastically *shifting gears* too often.

► Update your long-term plans every few months. It is easy to get bogged down in the day-to-day operations of a new business and lose sight of the business' future. Always have a vision of where you would like the business to be in three to five years, and what strategies you will employ—currently and in the future—to move it in that direction.

As a final suggestion, keep doing your homework. You might have scouted the competition, conducted focus groups and rummaged though census data in the library before going into business, but much of the information gathered may soon be out of date. In this sense, the planning process never really ends. The review and control step will lead to a new situation analysis, to re-evaluate your personal and business objectives, possibly redefining your business, reformulating your strategies and objectives, and writing a new document, which you will later review and revise to reinitiate the continuous planning process.

ASK YOURSELF

► Why do some entrepreneurs prepare elaborate plans, but fail to implement the plans?

► How many copies of your business plan will be needed (i.e., who will read the plan)?

► What is meant by the term "control"?

CHAPTER FIFTEEN

SECURING

THE CAPITAL

YOU NEED

FINANCE THE BUSINESS

A few budding entrepreneurs are able to finance a business themselves. Most need to locate at least partial funding. Unfortunately, obtaining funds to start a new business is usually more difficult and more involved than obtaining a personal loan for a home improvement project or to purchase a new car.

You will want to address the following three key questions to formulate a strategy to secure the capital you need: (1) How much money do you need? (2) What kind of money do you need? (3) Where can you find the money?

HOW MUCH MONEY?

There is considerable variation in the capital required to start a new business. Do not approach bankers or investors hoping they will know how much money you need. According to the National Federation of Independent Business, about 30 percent of the small business start-ups in 1987 required an initial investment of less than $10,000; approximately one of every four start-ups required $50,000 or more. In the fast food industry, Kentucky Fried Chicken was started with an initial investment of only $105. More recently, McDonald's first restaurant in Moscow, Russia required a total investment estimated between $40 and $50 million! Start-up costs for most small businesses fall somewhere between these extremes—like a Subway sandwich franchise for $75,000, or a Western Sizzlin' steakhouse franchise ranging from $744,000 to $1,454,000.

The amount of money you need for your new venture will depend upon the type of business, the size and scope of your operations, the location and specific site you select, whether you buy or lease the site and equipment, and most of the other business decisions you have made.

Fortunately, having already collected information for your business plan, it should be relatively easy to determine the capital you need. Refer to the *forecasts and budgets* section of your business plan and retrieve the data used to prepare your estimated start-up costs and cash flow estimates. Before finalizing your estimates, consider the following three suggestions:

First, avoid padding your estimates. Some *contingency* expenses are understandable and expected, but try to be realistic in your assessment of additional funds you need. Otherwise your potential lenders and investors may view your proposal as unprofessional, jeopardizing the likelihood of obtaining funding.

Second, do not make the mistake of raising enough funds to open the business without sufficient funds to operate the business once you open. Remember that cash is required to operate the business—especially as it grows—and that it may be several months or longer before the business is profitable.

Finally, determine the funds needed per stage in the life of your business. For example, if you plan to initially purchase your resale items from other manufacturers and not engage in manufacturing yourself until the third year of operation, the initial funds you need will not include production facilities. Many investors and lenders—especially banks—will be more receptive to supplying capital in stages, as your business develops and proves itself, rather than in a one-shot gamble.

WHAT KIND OF MONEY?

Rather than simply believing you need X dollars for your new business, consider how the money will be used. This will help you determine the type of money you need and the type of sources you should approach. According to John F. Murphy of the Small Business Administration, there are four basic types of money: trade credit, short-term credit, long-term credit and equity funds.[24]

Trade Credit

Trade credit is money the business owes to suppliers who permit you to carry inventory or materials on open account. You may have thirty or sixty days, for example, to pay the debt. In some industries, it is not uncommon for suppliers of seasonal

---

[24] Source: *Sound Cash Management and Borrowing*, Management Aid #1.016, John F. Murphy, U. S. Small Business Administration, 1984.

merchandise to extend trade credit for much longer periods, to help smooth out their production and marketing operations. Trade credit is an excellent source of financing, if you can resell the purchased goods or otherwise convert the materials into cash before the debt must be paid.

While trade credit is not borrowed *money*, per se, it is almost as good as a short-term loan in that it frees cash for other purposes. It has the added benefit of helping a new business build a credit rating. A good credit experience is proven evidence of your ability to repay borrowed funds.

Short-term Credit

Banks and other lenders recognize that your cash needs are likely to fluctuate throughout the year. If you are opening a retail store, for example, you may need more cash just prior to the Christmas selling season to build-up inventory. Short-term credit, repaid in less than a year, provides this type of money to carry you through seasonal fluctuations.

Long-term Credit

Such loans—for more than a year—are used for expanding or modernizing your business. They are repaid out of accumulated profits. Usually, the evidence of this type of loan in a small business is a mortgage or a promissory note with terms. A significant portion of your business' start-up costs may be financed through long-term credit.

Equity Funds

This type of money is never repaid. It is obtained by relinquishing a part of the business' profits to one or more investors. In other words, you would raise equity funds by selling an interest in the business. The investors share the profits, but also assume a portion of the risk in that there may be no return on the investors' funds if the business is unprofitable. Be sure to solicit the assistance of an attorney before entering into any equity agreement.

Combining the Financing Alternatives

When developing a financing plan, consider utilizing more than one type of money. For example, suppose you determine your *total* cash needs for the first year to be $100,000, of which $70,000 will cover initial start-up costs for construction, equipment, etc.; the remaining $30,000 is needed to finance inventory, accounts receivables and periodic fluctuations in cash flow. You might approach venture capitalists and long-term investors or creditors for the $70,000, try to establish a short-term line of credit with a local bank for $20,000, and negotiate extended trade credit with suppliers for the remaining $10,000.

WHERE CAN THE MONEY BE FOUND?

Methods to raise funds and potential sources of funds are limited only by the entrepreneur's imagination. Once you have done your homework and prepared a professional proposal, be prepared to contact more than one source, because you may face some initial rejection. This is especially true when the economy turns sour. During the 1990 through 1991 recession, for example, venture-capital funding for small firms dropped 66 percent. About 91 percent of surveyed small businesses felt a credit crunch, according to National Small Business United, and 55 percent of those who applied were denied loans for business expansion or development.

A list of several potential sources is included on the next page. Banks, venture capitalists and government agencies are among the most common funding sources.

Banks

Your banker may have gladly loaned you money for a new car or house, but may be reluctant to do so for your new business. It is up to you to convince your banker that you have done your homework and are committed to the new venture. Providing the potential lender with a copy of your business plan should help you to make a more persuasive presentation. When meeting with bankers, be especially alert to answer their fundamental questions, such as:

- How will you use the money?

- How will you repay the money?

- What sort of collateral do you have to back the loan?

- Are you trustworthy?

- Do you have the experience and background necessary to own and manage your type of business? What about your management staff and key employees?

- What are the long-term prospects for your business?

POTENTIAL SOURCES OF FUNDS[25]

- Commercial banks

- Commercial finance companies

- Venture capitalists

- Credit unions

- Customers

- Employees

- Equipment manufacturers

- Financial consultants, finders, advisors

- Founders and industrial banks

- Insurance companies

- Investment bankers

- Mutual savings banks

- Pension funds

- Private individual investors

- Private investment partnerships

- Relatives and friends

- Savings and loan associations

- Small Business Administration (SBA)

- Small Business Investment Companies (SBIC)

---

[25] Source: Robert T. Justis, *Managing Your Small Business*, © 1981, p. 156, Reprinted by permission of Prentice-Hall, Inc., Englewood Cliffs, N.J.

- State Business & Industrial Development Commissions (SBIDCs)
- Tax exempt foundations
- Charitable foundations
- Suppliers
- Trust companies (bank trust departments)
- Veterans Administration (VA)
- Venture Capitalists

Venture Capitalists (VC)

Venture capitalists generally make equity investments in smaller businesses with high growth potential. Many specialize in certain industries, geographic regions, technologies or investment sizes. The minimum size considered is often $250,000. Keep the following points in mind when you prepare to approach venture capitalists:

- A typical VC may receive thirty or more funding proposals or business plans per day; they will only read 10 percent of these. Of those they read, only a few will be investigated further, and even fewer will be funded. Therefore:

  - Make sure your business plan is professional-looking, written clearly and concisely. Some VCs believe an initial proposal should not be longer than twelve pages. Forty pages should probably be the absolute maximum. *Elements of a Venture Proposal*, on the following page, outlines the elements of a venture proposal.

  - Stress your capabilities and those of the management team. VCs generally feel they are investing in you as much, or more, as in your business.

  - Try to get an introduction to the VC before s/he receives the proposal. This might be arranged through your lawyer, accountant or other contact, and can be a definite plus.

- Have a stock liquidation plan prepared so the VC will know how to exit from his or her investment in your business. Most VCs want to invest in ventures with high growth potential—say, 30 percent annually—and then be able to *get out* in five to ten years—or sooner—before the business matures.

- Services such as the Venture Capital Network at the University of New Hampshire help link entrepreneurs with potential private investors and VCs.

Elements of a Venture Proposal[26]

Purpose and Objectives—a summary of the what and why of the project.

Proposed Financing—the amount of money you will need from the beginning to the maturity of the proposed project, how the proceeds will be used, how you plan to structure the financing, and why the amount designated is required.

Marketing—a description of the market segment you have or plan to get, the competition, the characteristics of the market, and your plans—with costs—for getting or holding the desired market segment.

History of the Firm—a summary of significant financial and organizational milestones, description of employees and employee relations, explanations of banking relationships, recounting of major services or products your firm has offered during its existence, and the like.

Description of the Product or Service—a full, detailed description of the product, process or service offered by the firm and the costs associated with it.

Financial Statements—both for the past few years and pro forma projections—balance sheets, income statements, and cash flows—for the next three to five years, showing the effect anticipated if the project is undertaken and if the financing is

---

[26] Source: *A Venture Capital Primer for Small Business,* Management Aid #1.009, LaRue Tone Hosmer, U.S. Small Business Administration, 1987.

secured. This should include an analysis of key variables affecting financial performance, showing what could happen if the projected level of revenue is not attained.

Capitalization—a list of shareholders; how much has been invested to date and in what form (equity/debt).

Biographical Sketches—the work histories and qualifications of key owners/employees.

Principal Suppliers and Customers

Problems Anticipated and Other Pertinent Information—a candid discussion of any contingent liabilities, pending litigation, tax or patent difficulties, and any other contingencies that might affect the project you are proposing.

Advantages—a discussion of what is special about your product, service, marketing plans or channels that gives your project unique leverage.

Government Agencies[27]

The Small Business Administration (SBA) and other government agencies make funds available to small businesses. There are often strings attached. For example, if you can secure financing through a bank, you may not qualify. Or, you may find the required periodic reporting too bothersome.

Other key distinctions about government loans involve political criteria, sometimes used in the evaluation of loan applications. For example, Merrill and Sedgwick maintain that your chances for obtaining a loan are enhanced if your request is small, if you or your partner are a female or minority, or if your business will be located in a depressed neighborhood.[27]

For more information about Small Business Administration loans, call the SBA answer desk at 1-800-368-5855.

---

[27] Source: *The New Venture Handbook*, Ronald E. Merrill and Henry D. Sedgwick, American Management Association, 1987.

Other Funding Sources

Other funding possibilities abound. For example, many franchisors offer attractive financing plans or will otherwise help new franchisees to arrange partial financing. It is in the franchisor's best interest to help prospective franchisees open new franchises, so ask them about financing alternatives they might offer.

A creative financing approach was recently employed by an inventor in Michigan. He raised equity capital from a group of investors when he agreed that if the business failed he would give them the rights to the technology he developed. Other funding possibilities are located abroad (e.g., there are at least 80 to 100 Japanese companies exploring investment opportunities in U.S. ventures).

Finally, you literally may be sitting on other financing alternatives. One small business owner from Chicago, for example, does what about half of all new entrepreneurs do. She uses eight credit cards with an aggregate charge limit of almost $25,000 to finance many of her company's day-to-day needs. Although the interest rates on credit cards can be relatively high, the cards may be a viable financing solution for short-term credit needs or when other pools of funds are dry.

ASK YOURSELF

► How much money will you need to start your business?

► What kind of money will you need to start your business?

► What are the advantages and disadvantages of obtaining funds from the major types of money sources discussed in this chapter, i.e., banks, venture capitalists, and government agencies?

► Which funding source is most appealing to you? Why?

CHAPTER SIXTEEN

CONCLUDING
COMMENTS

GOOD LUCK!

By now, you have probably realized that the phrase *small business* is a misnomer of sorts. There is nothing *small* about the quantity of hard work, skill and time required to make a business a success. Certainly, you are now convinced that there is nothing *small* about the laundry list of questions that you must address before venturing into the world of small business—the list of answers is even larger. I hope this book has not discouraged you. Rather, I hope it has challenged you.

After you successfully negotiate the obstacles to starting your business, the future awaits. Realistically, do not expect *small* challenges or *small* changes in the future. The world is not as stable as it was yesterday, and will be even less so tomorrow. Operating a small business will likely be more difficult in the future, unless you have done your homework and are prepared for the challenge. Consumers will have more choices, which means increased competition, but also opportunities to fill some niches.

To survive in *small* business, you will have to *work hard* and *work smart*. Winners will continuously re-evaluate the appropriateness of their business' objectives, strategies and mode of operation. They will anticipate change and adapt plans accordingly.

Once you take the plunge, it is essential that you are persistent. You must read, listen and observe. You must borrow ideas and insights and dedicate time to research customers, competition and the current outlook. A new business owner must not be afraid to pick up the phone and call for help, and to ask as many questions as necessary until the answers are found. Learning must be continuous. Most of all, as an entrepreneur, you must enjoy what you are doing and pursue entrepreneurship until your objectives are achieved.

Is small business for you? Do you have what it takes? Are you ready to break free? These are the last questions I will ask, but the first ones you should answer.

Good luck!

GLOSSARY

GLOSSARY

Accounts Receivable
Claims to cash on account which are expected to be paid within one year.

Agents
Middlemen that provide a risk-free procurement function by not taking title to the merchandise they buy or sell for their customers.

Amortize
Process of rationally and systematically allocating cost of an asset over the expected life of the asset.

Annual Percentage Rate
A credit arrangement term that applies to the relative cost of credit stated as an annual percentage, i.e., the annual cost of credit.

Assets
Probable future economic or income-producing benefits of value that are owned or controlled by the business. *Current* assets are those that can be converted into cash within one year.

Balance Sheet
A statement of financial condition of the business that provides the owner with an estimate of the firm's worth on a given date.

Broker
An agent middleman or wholesaler who arranges title-free sales for his clients.

Buying Power Index (BPI)
A composite indicator of consumer demand in specific cities, counties, and metro areas. Published annually by *Sales and Marketing Management* magazine, the BPI reflects disposable personal income, retail sales and population in the area.

Capital
Account that represents real ownership; it is the difference between the value of the assets and the liabilities. Includes owner's original investment, subsequent investments and profit derived from the business, less losses incurred and withdrawals by the owner.

Carrying Costs

Expenses incurred from storage of inventory. Includes interest, insurance, taxes, deterioration, spoilage, obsolescence, handling and warehousing.

Cash Budget

An internal statement used by management to keep track of inflows and outflows of cash transactions over a specific period of time.

Cash Discount

Price reduction or discount on bills paid early. Terms of "2/10, Net 30," for example, means that a 2 percent discount is granted if the bill is paid within 10 days. Otherwise, the entire amount is due within 30 days.

Collateral

Property that secures debt payment that the borrower pledges to the creditor. Collateral recovers all or part of a debt, if repayment of the loan is not forthcoming.

Cosigner

Any person that signs along with the maker of a loan or credit obligation, becoming responsible if the maker defaults.

Cost of Goods Sold

Determined for the specified period by counting the merchandise (physical inventory) left at the end of the period, subtracting its cost from the total cost of merchandise available for sale.

Current Assets

Includes cash and other resources that can be converted into cash or used within the normal operations of a business within a relatively short period of time, usually less than one year.

Current Liabilities

Debts and other amounts owed to creditors by the business entity, due within one year. Includes wages payable, accounts payable, dividends payable, taxes payable and so forth.

Current Ratio

A commonly used method of measuring a firm's short term solvency by indicating its ability to pay current debts from current assets. Current ratio is calculated by dividing current assets by current liabilities.

Debt/Equity Ratio
A measure of long-term financial solvency of a firm, showing the relationship between borrowed capital and owner's equity. Debt/Equity ratio is calculated by dividing long-term debt by the total equity. A high ratio might indicate room for capital expansion.

Debt Financing
Financing through borrowing capital that must be repaid.

Discretionary Income
Disposable personal income, less amount spent for necessities such as food, shelter, medical expenses, etc.

Disposable Personal Income
Individual *after-tax* income.

Double-Entry Bookkeeping
An accounting system where every debit made to one account has a corresponding credit made to another account.

Economic Order Quantity (EOQ)
The most economical quantity to purchase, balancing ordering costs with carrying costs.

Economies of Scale
Efficiencies associated with larger-scale operations. For example, it might cost a manufacturer $100 to manufacture one unit, $180 for two units, $240 for three units, and so on, such that the average cost per unit decreases as production volume increases.

Entrepreneur
An individual who organizes and owns a business for the purpose of creating long-term wealth. The responsibility and risk associated with the business are also the entrepreneur's.

Equity Financing
Selling partial ownership in the business to raise capital.

Fixed Assets
Business assets such as buildings and equipment that will be used over a long period of time—usually one year or longer.

Fixed Costs
Fixed amounts that do not vary with changes in the volume of sales or production, i.e., rent, depreciation, interest payments.

Franchisee
Affiliated dealers for distribution of products, services or methods in franchising, obtained by franchisor.

Franchising
Form of licensing by which the owner (franchisor) of a product, service or method obtains distribution through affiliated dealers (franchisees).

Franchisor
The business entity which provides the franchisee the right and license to sell a product or service and possibly to use the business system developed by the company.

Goodwill
An intangible asset that attaches to the successful operation of a business. Favorable factors such as location, product superiority, service reputation, and quality personnel often generate goodwill.

Gross Margin
(See Gross Profit)

Gross Profit
Also known as gross margin, determined by subtracting cost of goods from net sales.

Inventory Control
The process of maintaining sufficient inventory measures to meet customer needs, weighed against the cost of carry inventory, to determine an appropriate inventory level.

Inventory Turnover (or Turn)
Measures the movement of how rapidly inventory can be converted into cash within a period. Turn is calculated by dividing the cost of goods sold by an average inventory amount.

Liabilities
Debts and other amounts owed by the business to creditors.

Lien
A legal claim by a creditor on another's property, as security for payment of a just debt. May also appear as the result of judgment.

Line of Credit
A revolving form of credit where a bank loans a business up to a specified amount, as needed by the firm.

Liquidity
Ability of a business to meet its short-term financial obligations.

Long-Term Financing
Loans not to be repaid within one year.

Manufacturer
Business that produces goods for individual and/or businesses.

Manufacturer's Representative
Middleman agent who markets related but noncompeting products for several manufacturers or vendors.

Market
A specific group of people who have needs to satisfy and the ability to pay (purchasing power).

Market Potential
The maximum achievable combined sales volume for all sellers of a specific product, during a specific time period, in a specific market.

Market Segmentation
The process of dividing a heterogeneous market into several homogeneous sub-markets.

Marketing Mix
The four sets of tools the entrepreneur may combine to shape market demand and facilitate transactions: product, price, promotion, distribution.

Marketing Research
The process of systematically gathering, analyzing and interpreting data pertaining to the company's market, customers and competitors, with the goal of improving marketing decisions.

Net Sales
Dollar sales amount remaining when reduced by sales tax and any returns or allowances.

Net Working Capital
The difference between current assets and current liabilities.

Occupational Safety and Health Act (OSHA) of 1970
Legislation that led to creation of the government regulatory agency charged with responsibility for creating, establishing, administering and enforcing job safety and health standards in the workplace.

Operating Expenses
Expenses incurred directly with the sale of merchandise (selling expenses) and/or those expenses incurred in the general operation of a business (general or administrative expenses).

Organization
The sum total of the activities, processes and people that define a business.

Organizational Chart
A graphic description of a firm which identifies key positions, personnel occupying those positions, and reporting relationships.

Production
The continuous process of converting raw materials into finished goods.

Prospecting
First step in the selling process, developing a list of potential customers who have a need for the product, resources to acquire the product, and purchasing authority.

Purchasing
The business activity of securing goods or merchandise from an outside source.

Quality Control
Ensuring and effectively regulating the production of the number and type of goods manufactured to quality specifications.

Sales Forecast
Projection or estimation of sales, in dollars or physical units, for a given time period.

Secondary Data

Information that has already been assembled, having been collected for some other purpose. Sources include census reports, trade publications and subscription services.

Service Corps of Retired Executives (SCORE)

Consulting service composed of retired business executives that volunteer their management expertise to small businesses. SCORE chapters work with Small Business Institute programs in many colleges and universities.

Short-Term Financing

Repayment of loans within one year.

Small Business Administration (SBA)

A federal agency established in 1953 to assist prospective entrepreneurs in obtaining funds, and to preserve competitive enterprise in the economy.

Small Business Institute (SBI)

A cooperative venture between business colleges and the Small Business Administration that offers management assistance to small businesses.

Sole Proprietorship

A business entity owned and operated by one person.

Subchapter S Corporation

A form of business structure that limits each shareholder's liability (like a corporation). Profits and losses are reported by shareholders (like a partnership). Subchapter S corporations are limited to 25 or fewer shareholders.

Target Market

A specific group of customers at which a company aims its products and services.

Terms

The conditions or requirements set forth in a credit contract or agreement, such as a promissory note or installment contract.

Trade Discount
Reductions in price expressed as a percentage, from list or catalog prices given to a certain class of buyers such as wholesalers or retailers.

Turn
(See Inventory Turnover)

Unsecured Loan
A loan obtained without pledging any security. That is, no collateral, no co-makers, no guarantors, etc. back the loan.

Variable Costs
Are variable expenses that vary directly with the changes in the volume of sales or production, e.g., raw material costs and sales commissions.

ADDITIONAL SOURCES

ADDITIONAL SOURCES

No single book, person, government document, agency or organization has all the answers you will need to start your business. Consequently, you should consult a variety of sources after you read this book. First, contact your local library and your nearby Small Business Administration office (addresses for S.B.A. regional and district offices are included below). These two sources will give you the most *bang for your buck*.

If your local library has been designated as a *government depository* most of the census data and other government documents, statistics, reports, etc. you will need will be available.

The S.B.A. will be able to answer your specific questions about operating a business in your state. They will be able to refer you to the right agencies for information pertaining to any licenses or permits you may need. They will also be able to provide you with a wealth of small business bibliographies, booklets and pamphlets covering a wide range of relevant topics. Ask for their list of "Business Development Booklets, Form 115B," and their list of "Business Development Pamphlets, Form 115A." They may also be able to recommend new-business workshops held in your area.

Here are some additional specific sources of information you might wish to investigate:

S.B.A. Regional Offices

60 Batterymarch Street, 10th Floor
Boston, MA 02110
(617) 223-3204

26 Federal Plaza, Room 29-118
New York, NY 10278
(212) 264-7772

231 Saint Asaphs Road, #640
Bala Cnywyd, PA 19004
(215) 596-5889

1375 Peachtree Street, N.E.
Atlanta, GA 30367
(404) 881-4999

219 South Dearborn Street, #838
Chicago, IL 60604
(312) 353-0359

S.B.A. District Offices

150 Causeway Street, 10th Floor
Boston, MA 02114
(617) 223-3224

40 Western Avenue, #512
Augusta, ME 04330
(207) 622-8378

55 Pleasant Street, #211
Concord, NH 03301
(603) 224-4041

One Hartford Square West
Hartford, CT 06106
(203) 244-3600

87 State Street, #205
Montpelier, VT 05602
(802) 229-0538

40 Fountain Street
Providence, RI 02903
(401) 528-4580

Carlos Chardon Avenue, #691
Hato Rey, PR 00919
(809) 753-4002

970 Broad Street, #1635
Newark, NJ 07102
(201) 645-2434

100 South Clinton Street, #1071
Syracuse, NY 13260
(315) 423-5383

8600 LaSalle Road, #630
Towson, MD 21204
(301) 962-4392

109 North 3rd Street, #320
Clarksburg, WV 26301
(304) 623-5631

960 Penn Avenue, 5th Floor
Pittsburgh, PA 15222
(412) 644-2780

400 North 8th Street, #3015
Richmond, VA 23240
(804) 771-2617

1111 18th Street, N.W., 6th floor
Washington, D.C. 20417
(202) 634-4950

1720 Peachtree Road, N.W., 7th floor
Atlanta, GA 30309
(404) 881-4749

908 South 20th Street, #200
Birmingham, AL 35256
(205) 254-1344

230 S. Tryon Street, #700
Charlotte, NC 28202
(704) 371-6563

1835 Assembly Street, 3rd floor
Columbia, SC 29201
(803) 765-5376

100 West Capitol Street, #322
Jackson, MS 39269
(601) 960-4378

400 West Bay Street, #261
Jacksonville, FL 32202
(904) 791-3782

600 Federal Place, #188
Louisville, KY 40202
(502) 582-5971

2222 Ponce de Leon Blvd., 5th floor
Miami, FL 33134
(305) 350-5521

404 James Robertson Parkway, #1012
Nashville, TN 37219
(615) 251-5881

1240 East 9th Street, #317
Cleveland, OH 44199
(216) 522-4170

85 Marconi Blvd.
Columbus, OH 43215
(614) 469-6860
477 Michigan Avenue, #515
Detroit, MI 18006
(313) 226-7241

595 N. Pennsylvania Street, #578
Indianapolis, IN 46209
(317) 269-7272

212 East Washington Avenue, #213
Madison, WI 53703
(608) 264-5261

100 North 6th Street
Minneapolis, MN 55403
(612) 349-3550

Government Publications

U. S. Treasury Department
Internal Revenue Service
Washington, D.C. 20224

- ▶ Tax Guide for Small Business (Publication #334)
- ▶ Tax Guide on Depreciation (Publication #534)
- ▶ Employer's Tax Guide (Publication 15, circular E)
- ▶ Information Returns (Publication #916)
- ▶ Tax Calendar and Check List (Publication #509)

The Superintendent of Documents
U. S. Government Printing Office
Washington, D.C. 20402
(202) 783-3238

- ▶ Franchise Opportunities Handbook
- ▶ Census Catalog and Guide (published annually)
- ▶ Standards for General Industry (O.S.H.A. guidelines)
- ▶ U. S. Government Purchasing and Sales Directory

Useful Indices Commonly Found In Libraries

Standard Industrial Classification Manual
Guide that provides unique number, i.e., SIC code, for each
industry. Many other data sources are organized by SIC codes.)

Business Periodicals Index
Index to information found in business periodicals and journals.

Predicasts Funk and Scott Index of Corporations and Industries
Index to information about goods, services, specific companies
and industries found in business periodicals and journals.

American Statistics Index (A.S.I.): A Comprehensive Guide and Index to the Statistical Publications of the U. S. Government.
Very comprehensive source includes abstracts.

Other Useful Library Sources

Statistical Abstract of the United States
Contains brief statistical summaries from governmental and nongovernmental sources. Useful in preliminary stages of market or industry analyses.

County and City Data Book
Includes useful market statistics for cities, counties, and states in the U. S.

"State" Statistical Abstract
Separate volume published for each state, covers seventeen categories of statistics within the state: e.g., employment and earnings, banking and finance, crime and public safety, vital statistics.

Survey of Buying Power
Special issue of *Sales and Marketing Management* containing statistical data for cities, counties, and metropolitan areas in the U. S. Popular Buying Power Index is also included for each area.

Census of Retail Trade
Several census publications providing retail trade statistics for a number of industries and geographic areas.

Standard and Poors Register
Provides useful data and descriptions of industries in the U.S., arranged by SIC code.

Annual Statement Studies, by Robert Morris Associates
Useful financial ratio data for several types of businesses.

Directories

Business Capital Sources
International Wealth Success
24 Canterbury Road
Rockville Center, NY 11570

Canadian Trade Directory, Fraser's
481 University Avenue
Toronto, Ontario
Canada M5W1A4

Co-ops, Voluntary Chains and Wholesale Grocers
425 Park Avenue
New York, NY 10022

Credit and Sales Reference Directory
222 Cedar Lane
Teaneck, NJ 07666

Department Stores
425 Park Avenue
New York, NY 10022

Direct Selling Companies/A Supplier's Guide
1730 M Street, NW
Washington, DC 20036

Distribution Services Guide
Chilton Way
Radnor, PA 19089

Dun & Bradstreet Middle Market Directory
99 Church Street
New York, NY 10007

Dun & Bradstreet Million Dollar Directory
99 Church Street
New York, NY 10007

Food Brokers' Association, National Directory of Members
1916 M Street, NW
Washington, DC 20036

Food Service Distributors
425 Park Avenue
New York, NY 10022

General Merchandise, Variety and Junior Department Stores
425 Park Avenue
New York, NY 10022

Thomas' Grocery Register
One Penn Plaza
New York, NY 10001

Mailing List Houses Directory
P.O. Box 8503
Coral Springs, FL 33065

Major Mass Market Merchandisers
1140 Broadway
New York, NY 10001

Manufacturers & Agents National Association Directory of
Members
Box 16878
Irvine, CA 92713

Manufacturers' Representatives Directory
135 Addison Avenue
Elm hurst, IL 60126

Mail Order Business Directory
Box 8503
Coral Springs, FL 33065

Mass Retailing Merchandisers Buyers' Directory
222 West Avenue
Chicago, IL 60606

National Buyer's Guide 1980
115 Second Avenue
Waltham, MA 02154

National Mailing-List Houses
Box 15434
Ft. Worth, TX 76119

National Wholesale Druggists' Association
Membership and Executive Directory
670 White Plains Road
Scarsdale, NY 10583

Non-Food Buyers National Directory
1372 Peachtree Street, NE
Atlanta, GA 30309

Sources of Supply Buyers' Guide
P.O. Drawer 795
Park Ridge, IL 60068

Supermarket, Grocery & Convenience Store Chains
425 Park Avenue
New York, NY 10022

U. S. Government Purchasing and Sales Directory
U. S. Government Printing Office
Washington, DC 20402

Wholesalers and Manufacturers Directory
1514 Elmwood Avenue
Evanston, IL 60201

Trade and Professional Associations

American Entrepreneurs' Association
2311 Pontius Avenue
Los Angeles, CA 90064

American Federation of Small Business
407 South Dearborn Street
Chicago, IL 60605

American Management Association
135 West 50th Street
New York, NY 10020

American Marketing Association
250 South Wacker Drive
Chicago, IL 60606

American Retail Federation
1616 H Street, NW
Washington, DC 20006

National Association of Retail Grocers of United States
P.O. Box 17208
Washington, DC 20041

National Association of Variety Stores
7646 West Devon Avenue
Chicago, IL 60631

National Consumer Finance Association
1000 Sixteenth Street, NW
Washington, DC 20036

National Federation of Independent Business
150 W. 20th Avenue
San Mateo, CA 94403

National Small Business Association
1604 K Street, N.W.
Washington, DC 20006

Small Business Foundation of America
20 Park Plaza
Boston, MA 02116

Smaller Manufacturers Council
339 Blvd. of the Allies
Pittsburgh, PA 15322

Periodicals

American Journal of Small Business
University of Baltimore, School of Business
Baltimore, MD 21201

Business Today
P.O. Box 10010
1720 Washington Blvd.
Ogden, UT 84409

Entrepreneur Magazine
2311 Pontius Avenue
Los Angeles, CA 90064

Dynamic Business
Smaller Manufacturers Council
339 Blvd. of the Allies
Pittsburgh, PA 15222

In Business: For the Independent, Innovative Individual
J.G. Press
P.O. Box 351
Emmaus, PA 18049

Inc., The Magazine for Growing Companies
38 Commercial Wharf
Boston, MA 02110

Income Opportunities
380 Lexington Avenue
New York, NY 10017

Journal of Business Venturing
Elsevier Science Publishing Company, Inc.
P.O. Box 1663, Grand Central Station
New York, NY 10163

Bureau of Business Research
Box 6025
Morgantown, WV 26506

Manage
2210 Arbor Boulevard
Dayton, OH 45439

New Business
P.O. Box 3312
Sarasota, FL 33578

Opportunity Magazine
6 N. Michigan Ave., Suite 1405
Chicago, IL 60602

S.A.M. Advanced Management Journal
Society for the Advancement of Management
135 West 50th
New York, NY 10020

Small Business Report
203 Calle Del Oaks
Monterey, CA 93940

Success Magazine
342 Madison Avenue
New York, NY 10173

Venture Magazine, Inc.
521 5th Avenue
New York, NY 10175

Books

Accounting Principles, by C.R. Niswonger and P.E. Fess
South-Western Publishing Company
Cincinnati, OH

Beacham's Marketing Reference, Walton Beacham, Richard T. Hise,
and Hale N. Tongren, eds., 1986
Research Publishing
Washington, D.C.
(Small business focus with annotated bibliographies for each
marketing topic)

Creating the Successful Business Plan For New Ventures, by LaRue
Hosmer and Roger Guiles
McGraw-Hill Book Company
P.O. Box 400
Hightstown, NJ 08520-9989

Effective Small Business Management, 2nd ed.,
by N.M. Scarborough and T.W. Zimmerer, 1988
Merrill Publishing Company
Columbus, OH 43216

Encyclopedia of Business Information Sources,
6th edition, 1987 by Paul Wasserman, et al
Gale Research Company, Book Tower
Detroit, MI 48226

The Encyclopedia of Management, Carl Heyel, editor
Van Nostrand Reinhold Co.
450 W. 33rd Street
New York, NY 10001

Entrepreneurship: Creativity at Work
Harvard Business Review
P.O. Box 866
Farmingdale, NY 11737-9966

Essentials of Managerial Finance,
by J.F. Weston and E.F. Brigham
The Dryden Press
Hinsdale, IL

Fundamentals of Marketing, 8th ed.,
by W.J. Stanton and Charles Futrell, 1987
McGraw-Hill Book Company
New York, NY

Guide to Consumer Markets
The Conference Board
845 Third Avenue
New York, NY 10022
(Updated every 2 years)

The Guide to Understanding Financial Statements,
by S.B. Costales
McGraw-Hill Book Company
P.O. Box 400
Hightstown, NJ 08520-9989

How to Incorporate: A Handbook for Entrepreneurs and Professionals,
by M.R. Diamond and J.L. Williams, 1987
John Wiley and Sons, Inc.
P.O. Box 6793
Somerset, NJ 08873-9977

How to Really Manage Inventories,
by Hal Mather
McGraw-Hill Book Company
P.O. Box 400
Hightstown, NJ 08520-9989

How to Run a Small Business,
by J.K. Lasser Tax Institute
McGraw-Hill Book Company
P.O. Box 400
Hightstown, NJ 08520-9989

Information Bank for Entrepreneurs,
American Entrepreneurs Association
2311 Pontius Avenue
Los Angeles, CA 90064

Modern Retailing: Theory and Practice,
by J.B. Mason and M.L. Mayer
Business Publications, Inc.
Plano, TX 75075

Planning and Financing Your New Business: A Guide to Venture Capital
Technology Management
57 Kilvert Street
Warwick, RI 02886

Purchase and Sale of Small Businesses: Tax and Legal Aspects
by M.J. Lane
John Wiley and Sons, Inc.
605 3rd Avenue
New York, NY 10158

The Selection Of Retail Locations,
Richard L. Nelson, 1958
F.W. Dodge Corporation
New York, NY
(a classic)

The Small Business Index,
by Wayne D. Kryszak
Scarecrow Press, Inc.
52 Liberty Street
Metuchen, NJ 08840
(a bibliography)

Small Business Information Sources: An Annotated Bibliography,
by Joseph C. Schabacker, 1976
National Council for Small Business Management Development—University of Wisconsin Extension
929 North Sixth Street
Milwaukee, WI 53203

The Small Business Legal Advisor, by William A. Hancock
McGraw-Hill Book Company
P.O. Box 400
Hightstown, NJ 08520-9989

Small Business: Look Before You Leap; A Catalogue of Sources of Information To Help You Start and Manage Your Own Small Business,
Louis Mucciolo, editor
Arco Publishing Company
215 Park Avenue South
New York, NY 10003

Small Business Sourcebook, and Urban Business Profiles
Gale Research Company
Book Tower
Detroit, MI 48226

Strategic Planning for Smaller Businesses,
by David A. Curtis, 1983
Lexington Books (D.C. Heath and Company)
Lexington, MA

Who's Who In Venture Capital, by A. David Silver,
John Wiley and Sons, Inc.
P.O. Box 6793
Somerset, NJ 08873-9977

Miscellaneous Services

Bureau of Business Research
200 CBA
The University of Nebraska
Lincoln, NE 68588-0409
location research

Nielson Business Services
A.C. Nielson Company
Nielson Plaza
Northbrook, IL 60062
commercial market research

Reid Psychological Systems
233 North Michigan Avenue
Chicago, IL 60601
paper and pencil honesty exams

Venture Capital Network, Inc.
P.O. Box 882
Durham, NH 03824
non-profit service to match entrepreneurs with potential individual investors

Yankelovich Skelly and White
575 Madison Avenue
New York, NY 10022
commercial market research

ABOUT THE AUTHOR

Charles Martin is an Associate Professor in the Department of Marketing & Small Business Management at Wichita State University. Dr. Martin has been involved in several start-up operations including manufacturing, retail and service businesses. He conducts extensive research on a number of issues facing small business, especially those pertaining to marketing and customer service. To date, his research efforts have resulted in the publication of eight books and more than 100 articles. Dr. Martin welcomes your correspondence; feel free to write to him at the Department of Marketing and Small Business Management, W. Frank Barton School of Business, Campus Box 88, Wichita State University, Wichita, KS 67260.